Mrs. Entwhistle Takes a Road Trip

Doris Reidy

ISBN-13: 978-1-7329-9647-2

Dedication

This book is for all who engage in the hand-to-hand combat of authorship, particularly my generous and supportive critique group, the Verb Mongers. You are my tribe.

Other books by Doris Reidy:

Five for the Money
Some People Have Money. Some Are Rich

Every Last Stitch
Not All Children Have Childhoods

Mrs. Entwhistle
When You're Over the Hill, You Pick Up Speed

Imperfect Stranger
An Almost Perfect Fit

Mrs. Entwhistle Rides Again
Still Picking up Speed

Snapshots
Words Worth a Thousand Pictures

Contents

Acknowledgments

Cover design by Josh Langston
Cover photo by Edwin Verin

It's Never Too Late

"I'm under the doctor for the high blood pressure so I take these blue ones, and the little red ones are betty blockers--or something like that." Jacinta O'Reilly furrowed her brow as she shook her day-by-day compartmentalized pill holder under Mrs. Entwhistle's nose.

Jacinta was apt to get a little confused in her old age although, as Mrs. Entwhistle put it, she'd never been the brightest headlight on the highway. Now Jacinta paused to think, one finger on her cheek, eyes shut tight in concentration.

"The only Betty I can think of is Betty Jo Smith, who used to teach Sunday School. Do you remember her?"

Maxine opened her mouth to answer, but closed it again after a fierce look and a hissed whisper from Mrs. Entwhistle: "Don't go down that rabbit hole."

They were sitting in the day room at the Shady Rest Assisted Living Center. Mrs. Entwhistle and her best friend, Maxine, visited the Shady Rest every Wednesday afternoon. They were as old as many of the residents, but had been blessed with strong constitutions and resulting good health.

"Visiting is the least we can do; we're so lucky," Mrs. Entwhistle always said. But both of them dreaded it.

"It's the organ recitals that get to me," Maxine said as she drove them in her Lincoln Navigator. "You'd think they'd be glad to take a mental vacation from all their health problems and think about something new."

She always brought a book to read aloud, but seldom got through more than a page or two before someone, often Jacinta, was reminded of an ailment that needed discussing. In detail.

Mrs. Entwhistle and Maxine continued to visit despite their frustration. They knew how long the days were for the residents. Today Maxine had brought a book by Fannie Flagg that she just knew would be a hit. Instead, they were talking about Jacinta's pills again. Betty blocker, indeed!

Never the most patient of people, Mrs. Entwhistle was tapping her foot. Maxine watched with apprehension as the tapping grew faster and faster.

"I think it's time for us to go," she said, when she thought her friend had reached critical mass and was about to blow. "We'll see y'all next week. Come on, Cora, you need to let Roger out."

Roger was Mrs. Entwhistle's aged Shih 'Tzu, and it was certainly true that he needed to go out more often than ever before in his long life. Mrs. Entwhistle frequently had to get up during the night and escort the old dog down the stairs and out the back door. She accompanied him on these midnight excursions because she'd seen coyotes in the woods behind her house and knew Roger would be a mere morsel to such wild predators. She had perfect confidence that she, at age seventy-nine, could fend them off through sheer force of will.

Mrs. Entwhistle was uncharacteristically quiet on the way home. Maxine darted glances at her, knowing something was coming. She was not disappointed.

"Max, do you ever want to just get up and go?"

"What do you mean? Go where?"

"You know, just hit the road. Remember that movie, *Thelma and Louise*? Like that."

"I hope not *just* like that! They drove off a cliff at the end."

"Well, yes, but they had such a spirit of adventure. I think *I'd* like to have an adventure, go somewhere, get away from my routine and experience something new."

"What brought this on?"

"I guess it's being with the Shady Rest folks," Mrs. Entwhistle said thoughtfully. "I've known all of them for years. They used to be interested in other people and what was going on in the world, but now all they can think about is their ailments, medications and doctor visits."

"Well, when you don't feel good it does tend to occupy your mind, don't you think?"

"Oh, sure, I get that, but it's just sad. There's more to this world than counting your pills. I think I'd like to get out there and see some of it. One last time."

Mrs. Entwhistle sounded wistful. She and Floyd had never been able to travel as they'd planned to do when he retired. In fact, except for the trip she and

Maxine had taken to Hawaii, courtesy of her Publishers Clearinghouse winnings, she hadn't been much of anywhere.

"It's not that I don't love my home. I'm grateful for it," she continued, "and I'm not talking about a big elaborate cruise or anything. I just wish I'd seen more of the U.S.A. when I was younger. Do you think it's too late?"

"What, exactly, are you thinking of?" Maxine asked.

"Let's just pack up the car and take off."

"Do you have a destination in mind?"

"I'd like to see the Southwest," Mrs. Entwhistle replied. "You know how I love the book, *Lonesome Dove*. I've read it four times. Well, I'd like to see that countryside--tumbleweeds and pueblos and the like."

Maxine's face lit up. "I know! I have a niece in Santa Monica who's going to have her first baby in about a month. Her mama has passed. You remember my youngest sister, Lucille?"

Mrs. Entwhistle nodded. "Yes, that was sad. She was too young."

They were quiet for a minute, reflecting on the vagaries of life and how fast things could change.

Maxine's sister had gotten up that morning expecting a normal day and had a fatal heart attack. You just never knew.

"I'd love to stand in for Lucille, see the baby and maybe help out a bit if Lucy Junior needs it. I know Lucy will miss her mother so much when the baby comes."

"Santa Monica is near Los Angeles," Mrs. Entwhistle said. She pulled out her phone and conjured up a map with a certain smugness at being able to do so. Her phone had caused her many hours of frustration and confusion as she was learning to use it, so she felt proud of her competence now.

"You know what? We could take Route 66 all the way, like they did on that television show. We'd see some scenery, and the route is far enough south that we shouldn't get into terrible weather if we left right away. What do you think?"

The more they talked about it, the more they liked the idea. "We could take my car," Maxine said. "It's big and comfortable."

"The gas, though," Mrs. Entwhistle said.

"Yes, but we'll be splitting the cost." Maxine sounded defensive. She was sensitive about the fossil fuel it took to drive her behemoth of a car down the road.

"And my car really isn't all that inefficient. I only drive it on short hops, so of course it guzzles gas. But on the road I bet it would do fine."

"Well. Okay. We certainly couldn't take my car; it's pretty well toast. If I didn't have the scooter, I couldn't get around at all."

Mrs. Entwhistle had gotten herself a pink scooter as a result of her friendship with Dex Shofield, intern and co-conspirator at the hometown newspaper, the *Pantograph.* Dex cut an dashing figure on his motorcycle, and when Mrs. Entwhistle's old car finally died, he convinced her to try a Vespa. She loved it. She liked to say she rode her scooter with gusto, and if gusto couldn't come, she rode alone--humor that never got old as far as she was concerned. She knew her contemporaries uttered dire prophecies about what would befall her for riding a scooter at her age, but that just made the experience sweeter.

"Oh!" Mrs. Entwhistle was struck by a thought. "What about my job? Jimmy Jack counts on me."

Jimmy Jack McNamara was her editor and boss at the *Pantograph,* where Mrs. Entwhistle worked as a reporter--the oldest reporter ever, she suspected. She'd had some creative differences with Jimmy Jack, but over time they'd developed a working relationship they both respected.

"I'm sure he'd let you have a vacation," Maxine said. "You've been working there for over a year and have never taken time off."

"Yes, but I don't want just two weeks," Mrs. Entwhistle said. "I want an open-ended time to go wherever I want and not be worried about getting back for work."

"Well, you know what that means."

"I'd have to quit?"

"I guess you would."

"I need the paycheck, though."

They thought for a while. Then Maxine said, "Do you suppose the *Pantograph* would want some travel articles?"

~*~

It turned out Jimmy Jack was amenable to the idea of travel articles. He'd come a long way since the days when all he wanted to do was put out the paper with as little effort as possible. Mrs. Entwhistle had been happy to revise her initial opinion that he was indolent, indecisive, and ignorant. She felt the change in him was due to her, and harbored a secret pride that she'd brought him along.

"It might be just the thing to broaden our horizons," he said, when Mrs. Entwhistle broached the idea to him. "Most folks around here go by car when they travel. It would be a trip others might take, and so it'd be of interest to our readers. Do you have a planned route and destination?"

"Well, we thought we'd head for California," Mrs. Entwhistle said. "We've never been there, and Maxine has a niece in Santa Monica who's going to have a baby. She'd like to see the young'un and maybe help her niece a little bit. We thought we'd take Route 66, like on that old television show."

Jimmy Jack looked blank, and Mrs. Entwhistle remembered he was too young to have seen the program. "Never mind," she said, "It was about two young men who set out in a Corvette to drive across country on Route 66. Before your time."

"Do you think it's safe, though?" Jimmy Jack asked, worry creasing his brow. "I mean, the two of you aren't as young as you used to be."

Mrs. Entwhistle regarded him in frosty silence long enough to make sweat pop out along his hairline. "Not any of us are, for that matter," she finally said. "I think Maxine, and I are the best judges of what we can do."

"Oh, of course you are; of course," Jimmy Jack said, "I just meant..."

"I know what you meant."

"Well, anyway, travel articles would be great, just great. If you feel up to it..." Another frosty stare. "I mean, of course, you'd feel up to it. You could take your laptop and just send me a story whenever you like."

Mrs. Entwhistle took mercy on him and graciously agreed to file stories whenever the spirit moved her, while continuing to get her regular paycheck. Satisfied with the outcome of their meeting, she hurried home to call Maxine and tell her at least that aspect of their path was clear.

Roger met her at the door, his filmy old eyes searching until they found her face. Then he attempted a happy shuffle, but it made him cough, and he had to settle for wagging his tail.

"Oh, dear, Roger. What will I do about you?"

Paving the Way

Before she could come to grips with what to do about Roger, she got a telephone call from Dex. When he'd been an intern on the *Pantograph,* he and Mrs. Entwhistle had investigated and exposed a money-laundering operation going on right under everyone's noses. In the process, they'd become great friends despite the difference in their ages, and they still kept in close touch. He was finishing up his journalism degree and had a job lined up at the *Washington Post* as a result of their big scoop the previous summer. Mrs. Entwhistle could feel her heart expand every time she thought about Dex; she just adored that boy.

"Why, hello, honey, I'm surprised to hear from you

on a Tuesday morning," she said, delighted. "Don't you have class?"

"Yes, I do. I'm cutting," Dex's voice was an octave lower than usual.

"What's wrong? Have you got a cold?"

"Yeah, but that's the least of my worries. I need a time out," Dex said, with his characteristic way of getting right to the point.

It was so unexpected that Mrs. Entwhistle was alarmed. "What's happened?" she asked.

"School, grades, my brother's sick again, the *Post* job --the pressure's just too much. I feel trapped and exhausted and kind of crazy."

"Why, Dex, that doesn't sound like you. What does Lara say about this?"

"She said goodbye."

Ah, there it was. A break-up with his first serious girl-friend. The pieces clicked into place in Mrs. Entwhistle's mind.

"What can I do to help?" she asked.

"Well, I was wondering if I could possibly come and stay with you for a little while. My professors say I can continue my course work online. I was hoping you and I could just hang out together like we used to. If it would suit you."

"I'd like nothing better, but wouldn't you rather go home to your parents?"

"They've got my brother to worry about," Dex said, resignation in his voice. "I don't want to burden them with my problems."

Mrs. Entwhistle knew his brother, Alex, had special needs and that caring for him kept their parents hopping. Dex had learned to fend for himself growing up, and, as a result, he'd become an unusually self-contained young man. But she also knew even self-contained young men needed pampering sometimes.

"Honey, I'd love to have you here, you know that, but Maxine and I are planning a trip."

"Oh. Sure. I understand. Well, I'll figure something out. Thanks anyway."

Mrs. Entwhistle couldn't stand the disappointment in his voice. Her mind raced.

"But wait a minute, wait a minute; I've got an idea. What would you think about dog-sitting with Roger while I'm gone? He's really too old to come along, and he already likes you, and he'd be able to stay home, and I'd feel perfectly comfortable leaving him in your care, and you could get away from campus, and catch your breath, just be quiet, rest up and keep an eye on things here. Oh, Dex, would that work?"

"It sounds like a perfect solution to both our problems," Dex said. "If you're sure."

"Of course, I'm sure. Do you think you'd be lonely here by yourself?"

"Not a bit. I know a lot of people in town. I could always drop in on Mr. McNamara at the *Pantograph*, and there's Pete Peters, and Booger, and Caleb, and everybody at the Busy Bee Diner."

"You might have more company than you want, for that matter."

"No, I think it's just what I need. I loved it there during my internship."

"Now, you have to promise me you won't fall behind in school," Mrs. Entwhistle said. "You're almost at the finish line, and I just couldn't stand it if you dropped out."

"Never fear, Mrs. E., I'm not about to blow all the time and effort I've put in so far, not to mention wasting my parents' money. No, I'll finish, and I'll take that job at the *Post.* I just need some time to get my head straight."

"We'll probably be gone a month or so. How does that suit you?"

"Sure, whatever you want. Roger and I will be fine."

And just like that, a major snag was removed from her path. Roger would be well cared for, Mrs. Entwhistle's house would be occupied, and Dex would check on Maxine's house, too. They could leave with unworried minds.

But first, Mrs. Entwhistle would have to break the news to her children, Tommy and Diane. That might be tricky; her children were convinced she was the one who needed parental guidance. She still hadn't fully forgiven them for taking her car away a while back just because she'd had a few fender-benders. She'd had to take a driving class to convince them she was competent enough to regain her wheels. Never mind that she'd taught both of them to drive when Floyd said his nerves couldn't stand it. The memory of those early rides, her white knuckles clutching the edges of her seat, still made her breath come short. But Diane and Tommy had forgotten all that and now seemed to believe that she was a menace on the highway. Shakespeare put it perfectly: "How sharper than a serpent's tooth it is to have a thankless child."

However, this was not the time to chew over old grudges. She called and asked if they could meet her for lunch without the grandchildren. Much as she loved her grands, she was realistic about the possibility of having a coherent conversation with them around.

Tommy said he could make lunch if they met at a place near his office. Diane said she was busy all week, but she'd clear an hour for her mother if it wasn't on Thursday or Friday.

"I have yoga on Thursday and volunteer at the school clinic on Friday," she explained.

"Of course. Shall we try for Wednesday? The Busy Bee is close to Tommy's office. Would that be okay?"

It was agreed; they'd meet at 11:45 to get ahead of the lunch crowd. Mrs. Entwhistle rehearsed in her mind what she'd say. *Maxine and I are thinking, no, planning--I don't want to sound like I'm asking their permission--to take us a little trip. We're going to drive Route 66 to California. Wait, that sounds too adventurous. Better tone it down a little, bring in the grandmother aspect. We're planning to go see Maxine's niece in Santa Monica. She's having her first baby, and her mom isn't around to give moral support.* Yes, that would go down better with Diane. She'd surely counted on her own mother when her children were born. Mrs. Entwhistle had spent weeks helping with meals, and colic, and diaper rash. She'd been happy to do it. It was nice to have a reason to dust off the old skills, and, of course, she fell in love with each of her grandbabies.

For Tommy, she'd add, *We're driving in Maxine's nice big car; it has a lot of safety features, and we'll have our cell phones on us at all times. We'll take turns driving and stop for a break every couple of hours. We'll only stay in national motel chains, and we won't talk to strangers or anything.* Even in her thoughts, Mrs. Entwhistle had to cross her fingers on that one. She talked to everyone, and so did Maxine. That's one of the reasons she wanted to go, to get to know new people. But if Tommy bought it, so much the better.

Tommy and Diane listened in silence to their mother's announcement. She was careful to make it an announcement and not a request, much less a plea.

Tommy wrinkled his brow and stirred his bowl of chili. "But what about the cost? You're working because you said you needed the money. Can you afford a trip like this?"

Mrs. Entwhistle was ready for that one. "It's a working trip. Jimmy Jack wants me to write travel articles about the things we see. I'll continue to get my paycheck, and Max and I will be splitting all the expenses. I've saved up a little bit, too."

Tommy looked relieved. Mrs. Entwhistle knew he'd been worried about whether he should offer to help out financially.

Diane had a worry of her own. "What about Roger?"

Mrs. Entwhistle knew that neither Diane nor her brother wanted to keep the old dog at their houses. To be fair, she couldn't blame them. Roger was a bit of a trial these days, especially since he sometimes forgot he needed to go out until it was too late. He'd been banned from Diane's house after she got new carpet, and Tommy wasn't home enough to take care of him properly.

"Dex is going to be staying at my house taking care of Roger while I'm gone," Mrs. Entwhistle said. "So you don't have to worry or check on things. Dex will get the mail, and newspapers, and make sure everything is okay."

She noticed the flicker of relief in their eyes. Well, she understood. They were busy people.

"Dex? Isn't he at school?" Tommy asked.

"He's able to keep up with his school work on the computer," Mrs. Entwhistle said. "I think he needs a little change. Broke up with his girlfriend."

Tommy nodded glumly. That was something he understood. He'd broken up with several girlfriends since his divorce.

Mrs. Entwhistle motioned to Carol Anne for the check, which she insisted on paying. Floyd had never allowed the children to pay for a restaurant meal, and she wouldn't, either. She promised she'd let them know when her plans had solidified, kissed them, and hopped on her scooter for the short ride home.

Open Road

Mrs. Entwhistle prided herself on being a highly-organized person. Her dresser drawers were always neat, and her spices were in alphabetical order. It just made things easier if you didn't always have to stop and search for things. So she approached packing for a long car trip in the same spirit. First, she made a list. The usual things were duly noted: toothpaste, dental floss, eyeglass cleaner, charging cords for her laptop and cell phone.

Clothing was easy: seven pairs of everything, plus sweater, raincoat, and umbrella. If it got cold, she'd layer the sweater under the raincoat. But it shouldn't be too cold at this time of year. They'd be traveling through Missouri, Oklahoma, New Mexico,

Arizona, and Texas, and it was only October. She contemplated her straw hat and smiled, remembering how Dex looked when he disguised himself as her to deliver a ransom. The hat took up too much room and had no practical use on the trip, but she packed it anyway. Some things you just couldn't leave behind.

Maxine reported that she'd had the Lincoln serviced and bought four new tires. "The old ones still had some tread, but I didn't want to take a chance of us having a flat in the middle of the desert," she said.

The ladies debated whether it was worthwhile to try to find paper road maps. Those once-ubiquitous relics of yesteryear were in short supply in the age of Global Positioning Systems. Maxine's car was a year too old to have had a GPS as standard equipment, but she had an after-market one that perched on the dashboard when it wasn't falling off onto the floor. Their cell phones also contained navigational apps. Trouble was, they'd had bad experiences with GPS, having obediently followed directions into some scary neighborhoods. Sometimes, modern conveniences weren't all that convenient.

"I still like a good paper map," Mrs. Entwhistle said. Floyd had taught her to read maps many years ago, and she was vain of this accomplishment. "Tell you what, I'll take my atlas."

That book was dog-eared and outdated, but Maxine nodded. "You can't have too many resources," she said. They spent an evening planning their route with the help of the Internet.

"There are some things I want to see along the way," Mrs. Entwhistle said. "See here, this blue whale in Tulsa, and the Cadillac Ranch in Amarillo."

"Yes, and I'd like to see the Petrified Forest in New Mexico and the Indian pueblos in Arizona."

"We'll see it all; we'll have plenty of time to go wherever we please."

They grinned at each other like kids skipping school. Why hadn't they done this years ago?

Mrs. Entwhistle also had to get her house ready for a visitor. Dex wouldn't notice or care whether he had placemats and guest towels, but he'd need a comfortable bed and a place to do his schoolwork. She made up the spare room with her best sheets and gave the pillows an extra pat. Part of her wished she could stay home and enjoy his stay.

A sudden wave of regret washed over her as she thought of leaving everything familiar. Her autumn garden had never looked better. The red maple was splendid, and the asters were a cloud of color against the picket fence. Gazing around her familiar living room, her eyes lingered on Floyd's old recliner, the quilt her mother made, and the shelves of books she treasured. Oh, why was she leaving the home she loved to go traipsing all over the country? At her age, too. Why, anything could happen. What was she thinking?

I sound like the residents of Shady Rest. Next, I'll be recounting my ailments. The trip was my idea, and I won't back out and disappoint Max at this late date. Once I get going, I'll love it; I know I will. It's just hard to leave, that's all. Stop being such a baby, Cora.

She stocked the refrigerator with Dex's favorite foods, made sure there was coffee (as a tea drinker, her coffee supply was inadequate), and simmered a crock pot of homemade soup. Roger got one last loving brushing.

And then it was time to go. Dex's scooter roared up her driveway five minutes before Maxine drove in. In the last minute flurry of instructions, hugs, and excited woofs from Roger, Mrs. Entwhistle forgot her premature homesickness and got enthusiastic about the trip all over again.

At last, they were off. Seated on a plump new cushion, Maxine drove the first leg sitting as straight as possible so she could see over the steering wheel. Max was used to driving that way, but Mrs. Entwhistle thought it would be tiring to stretch one's neck like that for long periods of time. She was glad she was tall.

Road trips have a way of toning down the most energetic travelers. Mrs. Entwhistle remembered how it was when she and Floyd packed up the family for their annual excursion to the seashore. Diane and Tommy would literally be kicking their way down the road, too excited to keep their feet still. But after a while, the drone of tires on pavement and the blur of scenery past the windows cast a hypnotic spell over all of them. A gentle lassitude quieted conversation. They stared silently at the passing landscape as they rode along. Even the imaginary line down the middle of the back seat that defined each child's territory didn't seem worth defending anymore.

So it was with Mrs. Entwhistle and Maxine. "Cora," Max said around a huge yawn, "there's a rest area coming up. Do you want to stop and stretch your legs? I could use a cup of coffee."

They'd only covered fifty miles, but Mrs. Entwhistle could see Max was sleepy. "Sure, let's stop, and then I'll drive for a while."

"I'm sorry for being such a sleepy-head," Max said. "Driving does that to me."

They pulled into a rest area with nicely maintained green space, picnic tables under the trees, and clean restrooms. Walking briskly to get their circulation going, they nodded hello to their rumpled and road-dazed fellow travelers. One mother was juggling a little baby and two older children who were not getting along. The baby was howling, and the kids were slapping at each other while Mom looked ready to cry herself. Mrs. Entwhistle couldn't stand it.

"Why, hello, you two," she said, bending down to look the two little combatants in the eyes. "Are you on a long trip? It sure gets tiresome, doesn't it?"

The children stopped slapping and stared at her silently. "I wonder which one of you can run the fastest," Mrs. Entwhistle said meditatively.

"I can."

"Nuh uh. I beat you every time."

"See that tree down there at the end of the walkway?" Mrs. Entwhistle pointed at it. "Why don't you race down there, touch the tree and race back. I'll be the timer."

Pounding feet replaced screams and slaps as the kids ran. Their mother surrendered the baby to Maxine, who could always get babies to stop crying.

Mrs. Entwhistle offered a word of encouragement. "It gets better. I used to travel with my two, so I know how hard it can be. Pretty soon you'll be looking back and thinking, whew, glad I don't have to do that anymore!"

The racers returned, red-faced and out of breath. "Well, now, I'd like to see the best two out of three," Mrs. Entwhistle said, "before I declare a winner. Ready, set, go."

They were off again.

"By the time you get back in the car, they'll be glad to sit quietly," she told their mother.

But the children fell into a noisy dispute about who was the better runner, and who cheated. It quickly escalated to blows, and Mrs. Entwhistle got jostled around a bit. Their mother moved in with swift whacks to their respective bottoms, then turned and glared at Mrs. Entwhistle.

"Thanks a lot," she snarled. "Now they're wound up and sweaty and stinky, and I gotta load 'em into the car." She swatted at them again as she herded them into the back seat. After Maxine gently handed over the sleeping baby, the mother jumped into the driver's seat and took off with a scattering of gravel.

"Swanee!" Mrs. Entwhistle said, chagrined. "Well, that didn't work out. I believe I've lost my knack with children. Getting Diane and Tommy to take some exercise used to help when we traveled. Guess kids are different now. Aren't you glad our days of traveling with children are behind us? By comparison, our trip is a piece of cake."

"Speaking of cake," Maxine said, pulling the snack sack from the back seat, "have a Twinkie."

Mrs. Entwhistle did. Neither would ever have eaten such a thing at home, but they believed trip food should be as decadent and unhealthy as possible. Energized by sugar and carbs, Mrs. Entwhistle hauled herself up into the driver's seat, adjusted the mirrors, and, with an unintended squeal of tires, exited the rest area.

"My goodness! This car sure has pick-up," she gasped.

Maxine nodded proudly. "Doesn't it, though?"

They drove for eight hours that first day. As the sun set, they began searching for a likely place to stop for the night. Nothing quite suited them. They hadn't wanted to be tied down by a reservation, but now they wondered if that was a mistake. They'd hit a deserted stretch of highway, and the miles ticked by, each one more wearying than the one before. Finally, Mrs. Entwhistle spotted a neon sign blinking "Patel Paradise" into the evening dusk, and she pulled into a scene that looked like a throwback to the fifties.

A courtyard was enclosed on three sides by one-story buildings with rows of doors under a covered walkway. Another blinking neon sign, "OPEN," illuminated the first unit, which they correctly guessed was the office. Inside waited Mr. and Mrs. Patel, eager to welcome them. It didn't take much imagination to surmise guests were in short supply at the Patel Paradise.

"Good evening," the man said, beaming under his turban.

"Good evening, Misses," his wife echoed, "we are the Patels, and you are welcome to the Patel Paradise."

Both of them smiled with very white teeth.

Mrs. Entwhistle smiled back. "Hello, y'all. Would you happen to have a room available? Two beds."

"Please to come, I will show," Mr. Patel said.

"I, too," Mrs. Patel said, leading the way with a

whisper of silk sari.

The four of them crossed the courtyard to a door in the middle of the corridor. It was opened with a flourish by Mr. Patel. Mrs. Entwhistle and Maxine entered and looked around.

The walls were knotty pine paneling, the old fashioned kind with a yellow-orange tinge. Two twin beds were covered with hot pink satin bedspreads that would surely slip off in the small hours. Matching satin curtains fought valiantly with the yellow walls, and neither won. In the bathroom they saw a huge claw foot tub and a heated towel rail. Everything was immaculately clean.

Mr. Patel named a very reasonable rate. With a glance at each other, they nodded. “We’ll take it.”

Mr. Patel scurried to their car to carry in their overnight bags, while Mrs. Patel extolled the wonders of the comfortable beds and luxurious soaking tub as she opened and shut bureau drawers and the closet door. When she could get a word in, Mrs. Entwhistle asked if there was a restaurant nearby. With a dazzling smile, Mrs. Patel said no, there was not, but she would be so pleased, so honored, if the two ladies would share their supper.

Mrs. Entwhistle was dubious about Indian food.

Spices didn't always agree with her, but there didn't seem to be much choice. She said they'd be delighted.

Conversation flowed smoothly at the table. The Patels were interested in hearing about their trip and about their life back home. They were especially impressed with Mrs. Entwhistle's career as a newspaper reporter.

In return, they told about their upbringing in India, the sacred cows that always had the right-of-way, the temple bells that marked the hours, their immigration to the United States as newly-weds, and their gratitude to be living in a country so ripe with opportunities.

All this was said between bites of butter chicken roasted to perfection, saag paneer filled with creamed vegetables, and fluffy naan. Mrs. Entwhistle had never eaten such food, and she started out cautiously with small portions. Then she accepted seconds. Then, shame-facedly, thirds. Mrs. Patel had made plenty, and Mrs. Entwhistle, a fellow-cook, knew she'd planned to get another meal out of the left-overs. Even with that guilty knowledge, she couldn't stop herself from running a piece of naan around the vegetable bowl to get the last creamy bite of spinach.

"My goodness, that was delicious," she said, with a discreet burp. "Excuse me. You'll have to give me your recipes. I'd like to make these dishes at home."

"It's good to cook for someone who enjoys it," Mrs. Patel said. She looked out the window, though it was too dark to see anything. Her face was sad.

"Don't your children love to come home and eat their mama's cooking?" Mrs. Entwhistle asked.

"We just have the one, our boy Sanjay. He is in medical school. At Yale," Mrs. Patel said, her back straight with pride.

"I guess it's a long way for him to come, then."

"Yes. It is far, and he is far away from us in other ways." Mrs. Patel's voice sounded shaky. She turned her head and surreptitiously swiped at unshed tears with a corner of her sari.

"Now, Anjali, don't," Mr. Patel said quietly. "We came to this country so any children we might have could get a good education and have a chance in life. Sanjay has an excellent mind, and he's doing exactly what we hoped he'd do. Everything else will work out in time."

"We are proud of him," Mrs. Patel said. "So proud! But he has changed since going off to university. I think...sometimes I wonder if he is ashamed of us. All his new friends, he says they are rich and live in grand houses. We have only the Patel Paradise, and we are thankful to have it, you understand, but it is not grand. We are not grand. Maybe we are not good enough now."

Mrs. Entwhistle didn't know what to say, but Maxine did. She covered Mrs. Patel's thin brown hand with her own. "Kids get that way for a while, but it's just a phase, and they grow out of it. I'm sure Sanjay has good values--how could he not, with such good parents? He'll soon remember the sacrifices you've made for him, and he'll be just as proud of you as you are of him."

"Do you think so?" Mrs. Patel's eyes searched Maxine's face.

"I *know so.* I've had the same experience with my son."

Mrs. Entwhistle blinked. Maxine didn't have a son. But Mrs. Patel had regained her beautiful smile, and Mr. Patel was beaming. Mrs. Entwhistle reflected once again that there was never a better friend than Max.

When they got back to their room, she got out her laptop and tapped out her first travel piece for the

Pantograph.

You find out things on the road that you never knew you didn't know. After a long day of driving, we found ourselves in an area that seemed bereft of places to spend the night. As darkness fell, we knew we were too tired to go much farther. The neon sign blinking "Patel Paradise" was a welcome sight, and we pulled into the motor court with relief. I highly recommend it to anyone who comes this way. Not only are the rooms clean and comfortable, the innkeepers, Mr. and Mrs. Patel, extended a very special hospitality. They invited us to have supper with them, and I learned I love Indian food--at least, the way Mrs. Patel cooks it. I discovered that hot pink satin and yellow knotty pine complement each other perfectly, and that parents speak a universal language of love, pride, and concern. If all of the establishments along Route 66 are like this one, we're in for the trip of a life-time.

Blue Whale and Black Leather

Missouri was a wide state. They neared St. Louis at noon with Mrs. Entwhistle at the wheel. She almost missed the sign for the bypass, and the horns of annoyed drivers accompanied her in a last minute swerve to the exit ramp. Interstate 55 ringed the city, but, to their confusion, much of it was in Illinois. They had a moment of panic when they saw the "Welcome to Illinois" sign, but decided to place their shaky trust in the GPS.

Mrs. Entwhistle found she liked driving Maxine's big car. She could see over most of the vehicles around them without the aid of the pillow Maxine needed. Her old car had never had the horsepower of this behemoth, and lately she'd been riding her scooter, which didn't go above thirty miles per hour. In this car she felt like she was flying.

Maxine seemed perfectly happy to surrender the wheel at ever-decreasing intervals, taking naps and reading when she wasn't driving. Mrs. Entwhistle envied her ability to read in the car. She didn't like to admit it, but she was prone to car-sickness and had to keep her eyes on the horizon at all times. When her children were young, they'd known she couldn't look over her shoulder to see what they were doing. Anarchy would prevail in the back seat until Mrs. Entwhistle pulled the car over to the side of the road and turned off the engine. She didn't have to say a word. Tommy and Diane were instantly chastened into quiet ridership. She smiled now at the memory.

"What would you do if I pulled over right now?" she asked Maxine.

"Why sure, honey, I can take over if you're tired."

"Never mind. Just thinking of the old days."

Maxine smiled and nodded. The old days were familiar territory to her, too.

Cuba, Rolla, Springfield, Joplin. Route 66 unspooled like a ribbon beneath their wheels. So far, nothing had induced them to stop. Until they saw the sign advertising the Blue Whale.

"That's in Catoosa, near Tulsa. Too far for today, but I sure do want to see that whale," Maxine said. "Let's plan on stopping there tomorrow."

~*~

When the Blue Whale appeared beside the road the next day, Maxine turned on her blinker signaling a turn. "Why, my land! Look at that, Cora."

"Yes, it's a big blue whale in a pond," Mrs. Entwhistle said. "It's...different, isn't it? Wonder what it does."

Maxine parked the car, and they stood in the parking lot regarding the unlikely sea creature for several moments.

"Let's go in the gift shop and see what we can find out about it."

The lady behind the counter told them the history of the Blue Whale with as much enthusiasm as if she'd never told it before.

"The man who built it, Hugh Davis, was the director of the Tulsa Zoo, and he and his wife, Zelta, also ran an alligator farm nearby. In 1972, Hugh surprised Zelta with the Whale as a thirty-fourth wedding anniversary present. Can't you just see him telling her to close her eyes, leading her to the pond and saying, 'Open your eyes now,' and there was this big blue whale! Don't you imagine she was surprised? Hugh made the whale himself, you know, out of pipe and concrete, and he thought it would just be for their family's use. There was a diving platform on its tail and a slide coming out of its head. But the kids in the neighborhood just loved it, and Hugh couldn't turn them away. Eventually, the whale became the centerpiece of the Davis' new attraction, Nature's Acres. They were an enterprising family, weren't they?"

"My goodness, they sure were." Maxine was totally into the story, her eyes shining with interest.

"But, of course, they got old, Hugh and Zelta, and they closed Nature's Acres in the late '80s. Everything got run down, but the local people wouldn't let the whale go. They'd patch it up and paint it every few years, and finally one of the Davis boys took over. You'd be surprised how many people stop to see it."

"Uh, the whale doesn't...*do*...anything, does it?" Mrs. Entwhistle asked as delicately as possible.

"Not a thing," said the shop lady cheerfully. "It's just a big blue whale beside Route 66."

"And that's enough; that's all it needs to be," said Maxine. "Thank you for sharing its story with us."

She bought a tiny souvenir whale to hang on the rear-view mirror and led Mrs. Entwhistle back to the car.

"Well, I've gotta say, I just don't get it, Max." Mrs. Entwhistle shook her head. "It has no purpose."

"It's kitschy," Maxine said. "Don't you think it's fun to come across something that has no redeeming value except it's goofy and original?"

"You know, I do, when I stop to think about it," Mrs. Entwhistle said. "In fact, that could be a description of us."

Around five p.m. they began scanning the roadside for a place to spend the night. Once again they seemed to be on a barren stretch of highway without much to offer. Mrs. Entwhistle was getting increasingly squirmy.

"Max, I've got to have a pit stop," she declared as they approached a ramshackle building set just off the road. The lopsided sign announced it was the Pigsticker Bar and Grill. Actually, the sign said Ba and Gr l because several of the letters had fallen off. It wasn't good to think about who was sticking what pigs, but Mrs. Entwhistle was desperate.

"This place looks sketchy, but it'll at least have a bathroom. You can get a cup of tea. Well, maybe it'll have to be coffee. It doesn't really look like a tea-drinking place."

Maxine surveyed the dilapidated building doubtfully. The lights had just come on in the parking lot, and they sparkled on the gleaming chrome of a dozen motorcycles.

"I don't know," she began, but Mrs. Entwhistle pulled in and climbed out of the car.

"I can't wait, Max. Go ahead on in," she said, hustling off with unusual speed to the outside door marked *Cowgirls*. "It's all those Twinkies," she called back over her shoulder. "I'm not used to 'em."

Maxine followed more sedately. When she entered the Pigsticker, every head in the small, smoky room turned toward her. She stopped, hand on her heart. She'd never seen so many long-haired males in one place. There were man-buns, pony-tails, and locks flowing unchecked on leather-clad shoulders. Everyone but her had elaborate whiskers. Everyone but her was wearing black leather with a lot of silver chains.

"Oh," Maxine said in a very small voice.

One of the most intimidating men got up and came toward her. "Come on in, honey, don't you be scared of us," he said, gesturing to an empty stool at the bar.

"Sit yourself down and have a drink."

He sounded so friendly Maxine felt reassured. Everyone seemed to be smiling at her. She smiled back. Force of habit; Maxine always smiled back.

"Oh, well, maybe just for a minute. My friend will be here soon." She seated herself on the stool and tucked her feet on the brass rail.

"Now, what'd you like to drink, honey?"

"Why, I guess iced tea, if they have it."

There were fond chuckles and a few comments: "Just like my grandma." "Aw, she's a sweetie." The atmosphere was sticky with sentiment. These men obviously loved their grandmothers; they couldn't be so bad, then. Maxine sat up straight and looked around her.

"Well, actually, I'd like a beer."

One beer was quickly followed by another. After that time seemed to slow down and speed up at strange intervals. Maxine wondered where Mrs. Entwhistle had gotten to and what was taking her so long, but her new friends kept motioning the bartender to refill her glass. They told her about their hawgs, which she learned were motorcycles, and about the road trip they were on, a trip they took every year.

They loved their families, they said, and their jobs as truck drivers, factory workers, and landscapers, but it was great to get together without any of those responsibilities and revisit their carefree youth. Maxine nodded, asked questions, looked at pictures of kids, dogs and wives on eagerly-offered phones, and drank her beer. Beers. When they all started singing, she sang, too.

It was into this convivial scene that Mrs. Entwhistle finally entered. Her face was noticeably pale, and she clutched her stomach with one hand. But her physical ailments were forgotten at the sight of Maxine singing and swaying at the bar with a lot of large, scruffy-looking men. Arms entwined, they harmonized on "Hotel California", and Maxine seemed to know all the words. Mrs. Entwhistle was reminded that Maxine was a dark horse and even after all their years of friendship, she could still surprise.

"Ahem," she ventured. No response.

"AHEM!"

"Oh, hi, Cora," Maxine said, turning her head slowly. Her eyes didn't look right. She grinned. "Come meet my new fre'ns."

"Yeah, Cora, come on over here and pop a squat.

Have yourself a beer, or d'you want something stronger?"

Mrs. Entwhistle wanted nothing at all, not with the way her stomach was acting. But it seemed churlish to refuse, so she perched on the stool vacated for her next to Maxine and asked the bartender for a Shirley Temple. The crowd erupted in cheers, and Mrs. Entwhistle's back was patted rather too enthusiastically.

"I swear, that's just what my Mama would always order," one of the men said, shedding a few tears in his drink. "Put a little vodka in that Shirley Temple," he whispered to the bartender. "It'll do her good. Bless her heart."

Soon Mrs. Entwhistle found herself swaying and singing, too. They ran through "Dixie," "When Irish Eyes are Smiling," "Thank God I'm a Country Boy," and then she lost track. When she looked at her watch she couldn't believe the time.

"Maxine! We've got to leave right now. We'll never find a place to spend the night if we don't get going."

"Wha?" Maxine seemed to be having trouble focusing. "Ish it late?"

"It's very late." Mrs. Entwhistle hopped from the tall bar stool, but the floor had developed an alarming tilt since she'd first sat down. A strong hand caught her arm and held her upright.

"I don't think you ladies will want to be driving," the owner of the hand said.

"We have to. We need to find a place to stop for the night."

"Now, don't you worry about that. You ever slept in your car before? That's what you should do tonight. You ain't in no shape to drive, neither one of you. We got blankets in our saddlebags, and we'll get you all tucked in."

The ladies were helped to their car and the seat-backs were lowered. Blankets smelling of exhaust fumes and tobacco were tucked around them, and the windows were cracked a few inches.

"There now, you ladies just close your eyes and have you a good sleep. We'll be here all night, and we'll look out for you."

Mrs. Entwhistle's eyes seemed happy to follow this suggestion. As she drifted off, the lead sentence of her next *Pantograph* article wrote itself in her mind:

Today we saw a blue whale and took up with a motorcycle gang.

Where Do Old Cadillacs Go to Die?

Morning sun and the growl of Harleys heading out were their wake-up calls. Raising her head, which gave an alarming thump, Mrs. Entwhistle saw all but two of the motorcycles disappearing down the road. The owners of the remaining two were coming toward the car with steaming coffee cups in hand.

"Here you go. You just sip you some coffee. We need to go on and catch up with the rest before they get too far ahead, but we wanted to stay until y'all were awake, and we need to collect our blankets."

Mrs. Entwhistle and Maxine were helped from the car, the blankets were folded and stowed in saddlebags, and both ladies were bear-hugged by their benefactors. Then, with a roar of straight pipes, the last of the motorcycle gang headed out on the open road.

"Good gracious," Maxine said, rubbing her temples and squinting in the bright sunlight. "How many beers did I have last night?"

"No idea," Mrs. Entwhistle said, "but I never in my life had a Shirley Temple with a kick like that."

They stretched their backs gingerly and walked around a bit while they drank their coffee. Neither was accustomed to consuming alcohol, and they were remembering why. But hangovers or not, they had no choice but to resume their trip.

"I feel so icky," Maxine said, examining her pale, puffy face in the vanity mirror. She found her hairbrush and attacked her beautiful white hair. Mrs. Entwhistle thought if Max was on her death bed, she'd brush her hair so it would look nice for the undertaker.

The ladies rolled out of the parking lot somewhat the worse for wear, but with rebounding enthusiasm for their trip.

"We wanted adventures," Mrs. Entwhistle said, "and that was sure an adventure, wasn't it?"

"Oh, yes," Maxine said, smiling to herself. "Oh, yes, indeed. It's a good reminder that you can never judge by people's appearance. Those guys were just as nice as can be."

"They sure were. Now we've got about five more hours to Amarillo," Mrs. Entwhistle said. "That's where the Cadillac Ranch is."

"Anything to see on the way?" Maxine asked. She turned quickly away from the window. "Oh, no, there's another coyote head on a fence post."

"Don't look!" Mrs. Entwhistle didn't like coyotes because of the danger they posed to pets, but she didn't want to see their dead heads, either. Ranchers around here didn't share her squeamishness. A dead coyote was a good one, and they hoped its fellows would be warned away by an impaled head. Mrs. Entwhistle suddenly missed Roger.

"You know, I ought to call Dex and see how he and Roger are getting along," Mrs. Entwhistle said.

Maxine was already punching in the number. "Hi, honey, it's Maxine," she said. "Yes, we're fine and having a ball. How're you and Roger doing? Oh, he did? Well, he does that sometimes. Just clean it up as best you can. Take him out a little more often. Yes, she's right here. She's driving, though, and we have a rule that we can't talk on the phone while we're driving."

"Ask him if my first article has been in the paper," Mrs. Entwhistle said in her carrying voice.

Dex heard, and he replied that Mrs. Entwhistle's column was the talk of the Busy Bee Diner.

"Oh, good," Maxine said. "You say Jimmy Jack ran it on the front page above the fold?" Maxine turned to Cora. "Did you hear that, Cora? Jimmy Jack ran--."

"I heard. Ask him to save the papers for me. Ask him if Roger's eating."

"He says Roger is eating real good and begging for scraps," Maxine relayed.

"That sounds like Roger."

Both ladies smiled in fond remembrance. "Chow hound" was a term that might have been invented for the little Shih 'Tzu, who thought he could eat like a Great Dane.

"What's that, Dex? Yes, we'll be going right through Elk City," Maxine continued. "You think we should stop there? Okay, I'll tell her. Take care, honey. We'll keep in touch. Bye-bye now."

"Stop where?" Mrs. Entwhistle inquired.

"Dex says he saw on the internet that there's a Route 66 museum in Elk City. Route 66 goes right through town; he says we can't miss it. It'll break the drive up a bit, don't you think?"

The National Route 66 Museum was part of a complex of several museums. The women walked around gingerly, getting the kinks out of their legs, then strolled through the Old Town, Farm, and Ranch, Transportation, and Blacksmith Museums. Mrs. Entwhistle yawned, still feeling the effects of her unaccustomed wild night.

"Bored?" Maxine asked.

"Just tired, I guess, although this isn't the liveliest place in the world. Let's go, shall we? We need to find a nice motel for tonight. I want to take a hot bath and sleep in a bed."

As Mrs. Entwhistle prepared to heave herself into the high passenger's seat, her eye caught on a bit of orange fluff behind the right wheel. She paused in mid-heave and stooped to take a closer look.

"Well, lookee here. Maxine, come see this," she called.

It was a kitten far too small to be away from its mother. Milky blue eyes and a stubby little tail proclaimed that this was a baby too young to be out on its own.

Maxine scooped up the kitten and inspected it closely. "I'd say it's no more than four or five weeks old," she said, stroking the shivering little back with one finger. "It must have strayed away from the mother and gotten lost. Thank goodness it's too small to climb up in our engine. We'd have shredded it when we started the car."

"Well, what are we going to do with it?" Mrs. Entwhistle asked. "Looks like everything here is closing up."

Museum doors were being locked and shades lowered as employees and docents called it a day. Maxine walked quickly to the last two women getting into their car.

"We found this kitten," she began.

"Yeah, the mother cat was a stray. She got run over on the highway yesterday," one of them said.

"Is there someone taking care of the kittens?" Maxine asked.

"They all died. We didn't know this one was still alive."

"Well, may I leave it with you?"

"No, I can't take it. I have dogs at home."

"And I'm allergic. If it's still alive in the morning I'll call Animal Control to pick it up."

And that was that.

"Looks like we..." Maxine began.

"Don't even think it," Mrs. Entwhistle interrupted. "How can we take care of a kitten too young to be away from its mother when we're traveling?"

"I don't know, but we can't just drive away and leave it to die."

"Mew." The kitten's voice was a mere squeak.

They looked at her--somehow both of them were sure it was a girl--and admired her orange stripes, blue eyes, and miniature whiskers. Mrs. Entwhistle admitted to herself that she was cute. All kittens were cute; it was God's way of sucking you in.

Maxine wasn't thinking of heavenly tricks. She held the kitten to her heart, got in the passenger's seat and waited for Mrs. Entwhistle to take her place behind the wheel.

"We're not leaving her," Maxine said firmly. "We'll find a safe place for her, but this certainly isn't it."

Mrs. Entwhistle knew better than to argue when Maxine took that tone. She drove.

Fortunately, Elk City boasted a big box store on the edge of town. Maxine slipped the kitten inside her sweater and took her in with them. They purchased a small plastic litter box, a bag of litter, a pint of milk, and a doll's baby bottle. Mrs. Entwhistle added a can of red spray paint. Maxine raised her eyebrows, but was too preoccupied with kitten care to ask questions.

"I don't think she'll be allowed in the motel," Mrs. Entwhistle said as she pulled into a Best Western.

"What they don't know won't hurt them. Ask for a ground floor room in the back."

Once installed in their room, Maxine set up the kitten accoutrements and placed the small bundle of fur in the litter box. The kitten sat there looking dazed. Maxine picked her up and tried to feed her with the doll's bottle, but the milk dribbled out of her mouth. She didn't seem to know how to drink. Mrs. Entwhistle had a bad feeling they were heading for heartbreak, but she didn't say anything. No point, when Maxine had that determined look on her face.

"Let's name her Marty," Maxine said, "after Martin Milner, who was in the television show *Route 66*.

Marty could be a name for a boy or a girl, in case she turns out to be a boy."

Mrs. Entwhistle doubted the wisdom of naming a kitten so obviously on her way to Cat Heaven, but she nodded. It wouldn't matter much longer. Surprisingly, Marty was still alive the next morning. When Maxine tried to bottle feed her again, she managed a few weak swallows of milk and Maxine took that as a major victory.

"I think we should find a vet here in Elk City and get her checked out," Mrs. Entwhistle said. Maxine agreed.

The young vet who was available at the local clinic was called Dr. Carroway. Mrs. Entwhistle and Maxine were used to medical professionals looking like their grandchildren, and he was no exception. They tried not to hold his ginger peach-fuzz mustache against him. He carefully examined the minute feline scrap and asked how old the kitten was.

"We don't know. We found her under our car in a parking lot. Maybe four or five weeks? The lady at the museum said the mother cat got run over on the road."

"I'd say she's about four weeks old and obviously

suffering from separation from her mother. She was too young to be weaned and then went for some time without food or nurture. She might survive with expert care and a lot of luck, but the odds are not in her favor. What do you plan to do with her?"

"I guess we'll have to take her with us," Maxine said slowly. "We're on vacation, driving Route 66 to California and then back home. We'll be on the road a while."

"She'll die if you do that." Dr. Carroway didn't mince words. "Leave her here with me, and I'll do my best to pull her through. If she makes it, you can pick her up on your way home."

"That would be best, Max," Mrs. Entwhistle said. "If you're sure you want to keep her."

"I do."

Arrangements were made, phone numbers exchanged, and a deposit paid before the two set off again on Route 66.

"I hate to leave her." Maxine sounded wistful.

"Well, you'd hate it worse if we had to dispose of a dead kitten on the road," Mrs. Entwhistle said in a no-nonsense voice. Sometimes she had to be direct with Maxine, who was inclined to let her heart rule her head.

"Now let's get on to that Cadillac Ranch," she added. "Thank goodness, it hasn't rained lately. Much as I want to see those cars, I don't know that I'd wade through mud."

"No walkways?"

"I don't think so. From what I've read, the Cadillac Ranch is an art installation done in 1974 by a San Francisco group called the Ant Farm. They had a Texas partner who financed the whole thing, which is simply ten Cadillacs buried nose down in the dirt. People have stripped them down to skeletons, but visitors still spray-paint what's left."

"Aha! So that's why you bought the red spray-paint."

"Yep. Unique experience of a lifetime, is how I see it," Mrs. Entwhistle said with a grin.

Suddenly, there they were: ten almost unrecognizable car chassis stuck up in the air. Their distinctive tail fins were long gone and not much else remained, either. But people were picking their way through the barren field, and a cloud of spray-paint surrounded the truncated cars. Mrs. Entwhistle shook her can of red paint and waded into the nearest group. There was such a mist of different colors in the air she feared she'd emerge looking like a paint store card, but she wasn't going to miss this. Maxine watched from a safe distance.

When Mrs. Entwhistle had emptied her spray can, she walked the length of the display listening to the polyglot of languages. Tourists had come from all corners of the world, and the most enthusiastic sprayers were from Europe. She glanced back at Maxine from time to time and saw that she was talking to a man. Well, that was Maxine; she'd talk to a stump. No doubt she'd have a new friend by the time Mrs. Entwhistle rejoined her.

But Maxine didn't look happy with the conversation. Mrs. Entwhistle recognized a certain fluttering of the hands that always signaled discomfort. As she approached, she heard Maxine say, "I don't know where we'll stop next. We don't really have a set schedule. We might be going in a different direction than you need to go."

She looked up with relief when she saw Mrs. Entwhistle. "Cora, this young man's name is Downy Drake. Mr. Drake, Cora Entwhistle."

Mrs. Entwhistle willed her eyebrows not to rise. "Hello, Mr. Drake," she said, putting out her hand.

"Just call me Downy," the young man said, taking her hand in a limp, clammy grip.

Mrs. Entwhistle unobtrusively wiped her hand on the side of her skirt. "How did you come by a name like Downy?"

"Well, our name is Drake, and when I was little my mama always said I was as downy as a duck. It's silly, I know, but that's what everybody calls me."

"I guess it could have been worse. You can be glad you aren't Downy Duck."

He laughed a little too eagerly and shot her an exaggerated wink. "Yes, ma'am, that's a good one. I was just asking this nice lady if ya'll would have room for me in that big car of yours. I need to get on down the road; it doesn't matter too much where."

It was the wink that sealed Downy's fate. Mrs. Entwhistle disliked being patronized. "No," she said firmly. "We don't pick up hitchhikers."

"Well, you ain't exactly picking me up, are you? I'm right here. You know me." Downy's practiced boyish grin didn't set well with Mrs. Entwhistle, either.

"I'm sure you're a very nice person, Downy, but we *don't* know you. Sorry, but I have to say no. Good luck in your travels."

She noticed an ugly look cross Downy's face. It was gone in an instant, but it told her all she needed to know. She inclined her head toward the car. "Come on, Max, let's go."

Maxine, clearly relieved to be taken out of the decision, allowed herself to be herded back to the car where Mrs. Entwhistle installed herself behind the driver's seat and made a speedy exit.

"I feel bad," Maxine started.

But Mrs. Entwhistle was having none of it. "You'd feel worse if we picked up a serial killer."

"It's just that he was all alone."

"Was he? We don't know that. He could have a friend or accomplice waiting out of sight. We're two old ladies traveling alone. We can't be too careful."

"I know; you're right." Maxine was resigned. Mrs. Entwhistle's forcefulness was familiar, and Max had to admit she was correct, as usual.

The scenery wasn't inspiring. They agreed a person can only look at so many flat brown acres without getting sleepy, and they both found their heads nodding after an hour or so. This was more concerning in Mrs. Entwhistle's case since she was driving.

"We've still got a ways to Tucumcari," she said, pulling over. "I need to take a power nap, and I think you do, too. Let's just stop here for a few minutes."

She left the car running for the air-conditioning, pressed the automatic door locks and reclined her seat. In a minute she was asleep. Maxine regarded her drowsily, jealous of her ability to drop into sleep so easily. But in a moment, gentle snores filled the car as she, too, slept. The wind from passing trucks rocked the car like a cradle, and the radio sang a quiet lullaby.

In fifteen minutes, Mrs. Entwhistle raised her head and ran her hand over her face. Her eyes were alert, and she felt as rested as if she'd had a good night's sleep. Up came her seat-back. She regained the highway so smoothly that Maxine didn't even stir.

Mrs. Entwhistle sang softly. "Twelve more miles to Tucumcari, I've been hurrying there, to the gal I'm going to marry, with the yellowest hair."

In her mind, she wrote that day's column. *If you ever wanted to spray paint a Cadillac, have I got a place for you. Located near Amarillo, Texas, the Cadillac Ranch is nothing more than a bunch of old Caddys buried nose down in the dirt. But what goes on around them is not to be missed. You'll hear foreign tongues and see sunburned tourists of every nationality while getting slightly high on paint fumes. What inspires perfectly normal people to pull off the road at this particular spot? Why, the chance to shake up a can of paint, and let fly! Maybe we've all got that seventh-grade self lurking inside us, because a peculiar sort of community emerges along with the graffiti. You may be thinking it's not your cup of tea; all I can say is, try it. You'll like it.*

Her train of thought was derailed by the gentle SSSSSS from the rear driver's side tire. It couldn't have sounded more sinister if it had been a snake.

Downy Drake Returns

Mrs. Entwhistle heard the thwap-thwap of loose tread and pulled over to the side of the road. The sun was setting and shadows were flinging themselves across the pavement in lengthening strides. In the dusk, the highway seemed to be set in a moonscape of bleak, uninhabited land.

Maxine woke and sat up in the passenger seat. "What's happening?"

"We've got a flat," Mrs. Entwhistle said.

"But these are new tires. I just had them put on before we left so something like this *wouldn't* happen."

"Well, let's take a look."

It didn't take a master mechanic to see that a long nail sticking out of the tire was the cause of the problem.

"Wonder where that came from," Mrs. Entwhistle said. "I guess there's a spare, right?"

"Oh, sure, but it's under the back deck. We'll have to take everything out to get to it. Let's just call AAA and wait for assistance."

Mrs. Entwhistle checked her phone. "No cell service," she said. "We're out in the middle of nowhere."

"Do you know how to change a tire? I don't," Maxine said.

"I know the theory," Mrs. Entwhistle said grimly. "Floyd taught me how, but I haven't done it in years. The procedure can't have changed much, though."

She popped the rear hatch and began pulling things out, blessing the day they'd decided to pack light. Two big suitcases, two small duffle bags, a cooler heavy with ice and cans of soda, and assorted parcels and bags were soon lined up along the roadside. Beneath the deck she found a skinny donut tire that didn't look like it could hold the weight of the car.

"But it can," Maxine assured her. "The guy at the tire store said you can drive as far as fifty miles on that skinny tire if you go slowly."

"Let's hope he's right," Mrs. Entwhistle said. A compact plastic container held the jack. It had obviously been modeled after a Chinese puzzle. Getting it out of the casing had both ladies swearing. By the time they figured out how to put it together their struggles had become funny, and they were both laughing helplessly.

"Let's just drive on the flat," Maxine suggested, wiping tears from her eyes.

"We'd ruin the wheel," Mrs. Entwhistle said, "and that's expensive to replace. No, we'll just keep trying until we get it right."

The jack had never been used before and still retained a set of written instructions. She read them aloud, squinting at the tiny print in the fading light. Then she positioned the jack and turned the handle a quarter turn as directed. Miraculously, the big car rose infinitesimally. She kept turning; sure enough, the wheel left the ground. Maxine pumped her fist in the air and did a little victory dance. Mrs. Entwhistle fitted the wrench around one of the lugs and exerted pressure.

"Wow! Stuck tight."

She tried again--nothing. She put her full weight on the wrench and took a spill in the dust when it slipped off the nut. By now, she was panting. The temperature was dropping as fast as the setting sun, but she'd worked up a sweat.

"It's getting dark," Maxine said, as if Mrs. Entwhistle needed to be told. "Here, let me try that wrench."

But Maxine had no success, either. "The tire place fastens those things with a hydraulic wrench. We're not going to get them loose," she said.

They looked at each other in despair. "I guess someone will stop and help us, sooner or later."

A car immediately came into view, and the ladies stood beside the road hopefully. But the driver didn't stop or even slow down. The whoosh of his passing blew their hair back and stung their eyes with dust.

"The next one will stop," Mrs. Entwhistle said, trying to put confidence into her voice. In the distance they heard a noisy engine beating its way toward them. "Here comes someone now."

They strained their eyes to see the approaching vehicle. It was an old pickup truck, the original red paint faded to pink. It slowed and rolled to a stop behind their car. Two young men jumped out.

"Well, look who it is," one of them said. "I believe we've met."

It was Downy Drake.

"You can just leave me right here," he said to the driver. "I know these ladies, and they'll be happy to give me a ride. Thanks for the lift."

The other young man shrugged, got back in his truck, flipped his hand in a desultory wave, and took off. Maxine and Mrs. Entwhistle didn't watch his taillights disappear. Their eyes were glued on Downy Drake.

"Now then, ladies, what seems to be the trouble?" Downy asked. "Pick up a nail somewhere?"

"As you can see, we have a flat tire," Mrs. Entwhistle replied. "I can't get the lug nuts loose."

"Well, 'course not, you're just a little old lady," Downy wore a mean grin. Apparently the charm offensive was a thing of the past. "Let me have that wrench."

He had to work at it, but eventually he got the old tire off and the skinny new tire on. Mrs. Entwhistle was by then resigned to giving Downy a ride to the next truck stop. She didn't like it, but there wasn't a choice. She started to climb into the driver's seat when a hand on her shoulder jerked her back to the ground.

"I'll be driving," Downy said. "You, what's your name, Maxine? You get in the front passenger's seat. You, you get in the back."

He still had a grip on Mrs. Entwhistle's shoulder and propelled her forcefully into the back seat. Her protests didn't move him. He slammed the door, narrowly missing her foot, and got behind the wheel.

"I don't know what you think you're doing." Maxine's voice shook. "You stop this car right now, and get out. We never agreed to give you--"

The blow to her face snapped her head back. Mrs. Entwhistle screamed and reached forward, but Downy raised his hand again.

"Both y'all shut up and sit still, or I'll hit her again," he said.

Maxine shrank as far away from Downy as she could and rubbed her cheek where a red bruise was already showing. Mrs. Entwhistle sat still, too, beating back the wave of panic that threatened to wash over her. Her mind was churning. No cell service, so calling for help wasn't an option.

Together, she and Maxine were no match for a strong young man, so fighting was out.

Maybe she could roll down her window and signal to a passing car. But when she tried, Downy glared at her in the rearview mirror and raised his hand. She hastily closed the window. She didn't want to be the cause of Maxine getting hit again.

Downy drove to the next intersection and turned right off Route 66. When he came to a stop sign, he turned left. Then right again, left again. Mrs. Entwhistle tried to keep a mental map of the turns in her head, but by now she was thoroughly confused. When the car stopped, they all sat in silence for a beat. Then Downy got out of the car and opened Mrs. Entwhistle's door.

"Out, and hand over your purse." He grabbed Mrs. Entwhistle's arm and yanked.

Scrambling to keep her balance, Mrs. Entwhistle found herself standing on a two-lane gravel road. She shook her head when Downy demanded her purse again, but it was there on the seat in plain sight, and Downy simply reached in and took it. Her cell phone was in there, and her credit cards, and cash. Now Downy had them.

"Take off your shoes."

Again, she shook her head, but a push between her shoulder blades sent her lurching painfully into the car.

“Now!” Downy said.

She toed off her shoes, and he picked them up and tossed them into the car.

“Now turn around and walk away.”

“But I--“

“No buts. You ain’t going along, old lady. The next time someone asks you for a ride, you remember this.”

Downy swung up into the driver’s seat, started the car and drove away. Maxine was yelling. Mrs.Entwhistle heard her protests cut off suddenly.

“Be quiet, Max!” she whispered. “Don’t get hurt.”

The car disappeared down the road. Mrs. Entwhistle looked after it for a long time. She had no shoes, no phone, no money, no credit cards, no I.D., and no knowledge of where she was. She stood in the middle of the road as darkness gathered around her like a shroud. Then she started walking.

Walking

There've got to be houses along this road. I'll find one, knock on the door and ask for help. Or maybe someone will come along in a car. Thinking of Downy, Mrs. Entwhistle decided she'd forego flagging down a driver. You never knew who you'd get. A house, a ranch, would mean family and was bound to be safer. They'd have a phone so she could call the police and tell them to look for Maxine. Her situation was dire, but poor Max had been kidnapped and was in danger. Mrs. Entwhistle was far more worried about Max than herself. She walked, scanning the horizon for the flicker of lights.

The gravel was painful to her bare feet, and it was too dark to avoid the sharpest rocks. When headlights approached at some speed, Mrs. Entwhistle stepped into the ditch beside the road to avoid getting run down. Her left foot hit a prickly pear cactus, and the needles pierced deeply into her heel, causing such pain that she hardly noticed the pickup truck zoom past her without even slowing down.

There was no hope of removing the spines in the dark. Tiptoeing on her left foot to avoid driving the spines deeper into her heel, she kept walking. She thought longingly of her cane rattling around in the back of Maxine's car, brought along "just in case." If she'd ever needed it, she needed it now.

With nightfall came a drop in the temperature. A cool breeze brought a sudden, brief shower. Mrs. Entwhistle was soaked, and soon she was shivering. She felt tears of fear and frustration threaten, so she began singing. The only song that came into her head was an old hymn she remembered from childhood church services.

Sowing in the morning, sowing seeds of kindness,
Sowing in the noontide, and the dewy eve;
Waiting for the harvest, and the time of reaping,
We shall come rejoicing, bringing in the sheaves.

She sang off-key in a trembling voice, but somehow the sound gave her courage. *There's nothing wrong with me that dry clothes and a pair of tweezers can't fix,* she told herself stoutly. *All I have to do is keep on walking. Eventually, I'm bound to get to civilization.*

In the distance, she heard the baying of a pack of dogs. As the sounds came closer and closer, Mrs. Entwhistle looked around for a refuge, but she was on a flat road in the middle of a flat land, crippled, shivering, and scared. She stopped singing in the hope the dog pack would not find her.

But they had her scent, and soon three big dogs sprang out of the darkness to circle her. Two of them hung back, barking and raising their hackles. One was quiet, approaching cautiously. Mrs. Entwhistle stood as still as a statue, balancing on her right foot and her left toes. She made no sound and avoided eye contact.

All her life, she'd loved dogs and studied them. She knew that a pack of excited dogs--even gentle ones--could be roused to group madness if their prey drive was triggered. So she stood still and submitted to inspection. After a minute, the first dog was joined by the others. They crowded around Mrs. Entwhistle and sniffed her thoroughly.

She ventured a hand to the underside of the nearest muzzle and was allowed to scratch a chin. Then a head pushed up under her hand, and she rubbed behind the ears. As the dogs jockeyed for position, she realized they were pets, accustomed to being handled by humans. Her spirits lifted. She'd been found. Now, with any luck, the pack would take her home with them.

Limping along among the dogs, she felt like she'd been joined by the best of companions. They seemed perfectly content to have her in their midst and stayed beside her on the road, aside from many forays to sniff interesting things in the ditch. The friendly dog who'd approached her even permitted Mrs. Entwhistle to lean on her a bit. After a while, the rhythm of the pack became her rhythm, and she found herself limping along quite ably. She felt almost like she was walking in her sleep, lulled by the utter darkness and her furry fellow-travelers.

Suddenly, the pack deserted her, racing away as silently as shadows. She saw in the distance a single light. The dogs were going home. She followed as rapidly as she could, hopeful that rescue was near.

The light was farther away than she'd thought. *In the dark, even one light shines for miles. I must remember that, it's a metaphor or something,* she thought. Finally, she made it to a packed dirt farmyard and stopped for a moment to survey the little cabin before her. A warm, yellow light glowed from an oil lamp in the front window. The dogs were sprawled on the porch panting and thumping their tails as she made her way to the door. Apparently, she wasn't considered a stranger anymore.

She knocked. Not a sound from within. She called out, "Hello? Hello? My name is Cora Entwhistle, and I need help. Hello?"

A face appeared at the window and looked her up, and down. *I must be a sight. An old lady with no shoes, knocking on the door in the middle of the night. No wonder no one's answering*. She heard a bolt being drawn back, and the door opened a crack. An eye looked out at her.

"What do you want?" The voice sounded young.

"I'm sorry to bother you, but I'm in trouble. My friend and I were car-jacked, and I was left beside the road. My friend has been kidnapped." She heard her voice tremble.

Maybe it was the tremble that did it, because the door swung wide, and Mrs. Entwhistle beheld a very young woman, a girl, really, in a state of advanced pregnancy.

"You'd better come in," the girl said. "Don't know what's the matter with these dogs that they didn't warn me of a stranger."

"I'm not a stranger to them. We walked the last mile or two together."

As Mrs. Entwhistle limped into the lighted room, the girl's face changed. Concern replaced wariness. "Well, my goodness," she said, "your poor feet! Let me get you a basin of warm water to soak them in. I bet you're thirsty if you've been walking; I'll bring you a glass of water."

Mrs. Entwhistle realized that she was. "That'd be wonderful, honey. My name is Cora Entwhistle. May I know your name?"

"Oh, sure, sorry. I'm Delilah Carson. Mrs. Carson," she added. "But you can just call me Delilah."

"I prefer Mrs. Entwhistle," Mrs. Entwhistle said with a warm smile. "It's just because I'm old myself, I guess, that I like the old ways."

"Jeff told me never to open the door to anyone I don't know," Delilah said, worry in her voice. "But I couldn't just leave you out there, could I?"

"Certainly not," Mrs. Entwhistle agreed. "I'm sure Jeff --is that your husband?--will understand. Will he be home soon?"

"I hope so." Delilah knelt awkwardly, supporting her belly with both hands. She lifted Mrs. Entwhistle's foot from the warm water and began teasing the spines out of her heel with a tweezers. "He went to town this morning in his old truck," she continued. "I sure hope he didn't have trouble with it. You didn't see a truck on the road, did you?"

"Just one, and it was going fast in the opposite direction. I had to jump in the ditch, and that's when I stepped on the spines. But listen, the most important thing is I've got to call the police and tell them about Maxine. Downy--that's the guy who stole our car--took her with him. He's already hit her, and there's no telling where she is or if she's okay. He took my purse; my cell phone was in it and all my money and credit cards, and then he took my shoes. Please, may I use your telephone?"

"We don't have one," Delilah said. "No telephone lines out this far, no cell towers, and no electricity."

Mrs. Entwhistle digested this dismaying news in silence. She looked around the one-room cabin. There were a couple of cabinets on one wall, a metal sink on legs, a pine table with two chairs, a bed in the corner, and a curtained-off area that apparently passed for a bathroom.

She asked, "Do you have another vehicle beside Jeff's truck?'

"No, ma'am."

"What would you do in an emergency? What will you do when your baby comes?"

"Why, Jeff always knows what to do. He'll take care of me, like he said he would."

"But he isn't here now."

"No. It's just me and the dogs."

Mrs. Entwhistle gently disengaged her foot from Delilah's hands and stood. "I've got to go on, then, and find someplace with a telephone. I've got to get help for Maxine."

"There's no other place for miles," Delilah said, "and you can't walk far on that foot. Best just wait for Jeff to get home, and he'll take you to town to the sheriff's office."

"But when will he be back? Maxine is in danger!" Mrs. Entwhistle heard her voice rise in panic. "I'm sorry, I don't mean to yell. I've just naturally got a real loud voice. But I'm so scared for my friend."

"I don't know exactly when Jeff will get back, but he'll know what to do when he gets here."

Mrs. Entwhistle knew Delilah was right, although she found it hard to share her child-like faith in the absent Jeff. It would do no good to go limping out into the night if there were no neighbors for miles. She was stuck here, as stuck as she'd ever been in her life.

Birthin' Babies

Maxine yelled her head off as Downy drove away from Mrs. Entwhistle. She hit at him with both hands, ignoring his orders to, 'Stop, dammit!' He reached over and punched her in the face so hard she tasted the iron of blood. She felt it trickle down her lip.

"Now sit there and shut up!" Downy roared. "Or I'll put you out on the road, too, only I won't stop the car first."

She sat as still as possible, trying not to cry. She knew Mrs. Entwhistle wouldn't give in to tears at such a moment.

"Where are you taking me?" she asked softly.

"I'm not taking you nowhere. You're just in the car. When I'm done with you, you won't be in the car no more."

"Please let me out," Maxine begged. "Stop and let me out, and I won't tell anyone you took my car."

"Oh, sure, 'course you won't." Downy snorted with laughter. "I reckon you'll just go home and get you another car and never say a word about it."

"I will, I promise. Let me find Cora. She's all alone back there on that deserted road."

"*That one.* She'll figure it out. Or maybe she won't. Doesn't matter, I'll be long gone before she can get help. I know that road; I grew up on it. There ain't no houses for miles, and there's packs of coyotes that hunt there, might even be some wolves, and rattlers, and no water holes at this time of year. Yeah, that one'll fit right in. She'll be just fine, and if she ain't, well, it ain't my problem." Downy laughed again.

Maxine shivered. She'd never heard such an evil sound. She sank back in her seat, rubbing her jaw and trying to think. What would Cora do? It was hard to be logical under the circumstances, but she tried her best. Cora would not panic, Maxine knew that for sure. She wouldn't waste her energy fighting when there was no chance of winning. She'd bide her time until she had a chance to signal for help or get away from Downy. Maxine sat quietly and made her plans.

Sooner or later, Downy would have to stop for gas. She'd tell him she had to use the ladies' room, and she'd find a way to leave an SOS in there. If he let her take her purse, she could write on the mirror with lipstick. If not, well, she'd figure it out. Maybe she could break away and appeal to the proprietor for help. She could scream and fight with Downy, make a big scene. Surely that would trigger a phone call to the police.

The miles hummed by. Maxine cursed the gas mileage that used to be a source of pride. The farther they got from where he'd left Mrs. Entwhistle, the harder it would be for her to retrace the route.

~*~

Mrs. Entwhistle, too, was marshaling her thoughts. She was stuck in the middle of a vast prairie in an isolated cabin with a pregnant young woman. She had no cell phone or vehicle. No shoes, either, for that matter. There was simply no way to summon help until Jeff returned. Maxine was presumably still in the car with Downy, going who knows where. Mrs. Entwhistle suppressed a stab of fear; she had to believe that Max was okay. Just scared and shaken, but okay. Downy wasn't a killer. If he was, he'd have killed her instead of leaving her beside the road. She'd hang onto that belief.

Delilah fixed her a cup of tea and offered a peanut butter and jelly sandwich, but Mrs. Entwhistle couldn't eat. The two women sat and looked at each other, equally at a loss on how to proceed. That wouldn't do. Mrs. Entwhistle took charge.

"Delilah, when is your baby due?" she asked.

"Any day now. I don't know if it's a boy or a girl, but I think it's a boy because he's been so active. Just the last day or so, he's really quieted down, though. Do you think that's a bad sign?"

"Hmm. I guess he's got his head down in the birth canal. They get quieter when they're in position to be born. Do you feel more pressure than usual?"

"I sure do. I have to pee like every fifteen minutes. Is that why?"

"More than likely. What will you do when labor starts?"

Delilah wrinkled her round, childlike forehead. "Why, I guess Jeff will take me to town to the hospital?" It sounded more like a question than a plan.

Mrs. Entwhistle shook her head. The poor child hadn't even thought that far. "Have you been seeing a doctor in town for prenatal care?" she asked.

"No, Jeff said I was healthy and didn't need to. He said he could tell everything was all right. He doesn't like doctors. He wants me to have the baby natural, like nature intended."

Mrs. Entwhistle nodded grimly. She didn't trust herself to speak. This child, about to have another child, was at the mercy of a man who somehow knew all about giving birth despite never having done so himself. He evidently thought nothing of going off for hours, leaving Delilah alone when she could go into labor at any moment.

All of Mrs. Entwhistle's maternal instincts kicked into overdrive. She remembered Diane's labor vividly, and the delivery of Mrs. Entwhistle's first grandchild. Diane, for all her independence, had wanted her mother then, and Mrs. Entwhistle had been present for the entire twelve-hour ordeal of labor and birth. Of course, they'd been in the hospital with nurses and doctors all around and pain-killers for the asking. Mrs. Entwhistle hadn't actually had to do anything except provide moral support. Her thoughts were interrupted when she noticed Delilah pressing both hands to her back.

"Are you all right?"

"Got a back-ache. I've had it all day. It's been coming and going, but now it just stays."

Maxine Makes a Break For it

Maxine woke with a start. The sun was up. How could she have gone to sleep in such a dangerous situation? She wondered if she had a slight concussion from those punches to her head.

Downy was pulling the car up to the pump in a tiny rural gas station. The peeling, hand-painted sign over the door proclaimed it to be Ridley's Filling Station. A large, whiskery man wearing bib overalls and cowboy boots let the screen door slam behind him as he emerged from the building and approached their car.

"What'll it be, mister?" he asked.

"Fill up. But I can do it." Downy wanted as little

interaction as possible.

"No, you cain't. You ain't in the city, son. This pump only works when I turn the key." He brandished the key as he spoke. "Now, you want me to fill 'er up, you say?"

"Yessir."

"I'll need to see your money first. I don't take credit cards."

Downy leaned into the car and fumbled in Mrs. Entwhistle's purse for her cash. While he was distracted, Maxine hopped from the car.

"I'm just going to go to the ladies room," she said.

Downy turned on her quickly. "You get back in the car," he ordered.

Maxine stood her ground, although her knees were shaking. She shot a look of appeal at the man.

"Seems like if the lady wants to use the facilities, she should," the proprietor spoke slowly, looking from the elderly lady with the bruised face to her young, nervous companion. "I don't believe in getting in peoples' business, but you ain't treatin' your mama very nice."

Downy shrugged sullenly. "She ain't my mama."

“It’s around to the side,” the old man said to Maxine, ignoring Downy. “The key’s hangin’ right inside the office door.”

It hurt her split lip to smile, but Maxine smiled anyway and hurried to the lopsided little office. She reached inside the door and found the key with a big cardboard tag that said LADY. Racing around the building to the side, she inserted the key, let herself into the tiny room and locked the door behind her. For the first time in hours, she took a deep breath and then wished she hadn’t. The whiskery man, whom she assumed to be Ridley, didn’t visit this room very often for cleaning purposes.

Maxine looked around her. The restroom was about four feet square and contained only a toilet and ancient sink. Both wore deep brown rust stains and dripped plops of water like metronomes. But the best thing, the very best thing possible, was a low, double-hung sash window. Maxine tried to raise it, but the years had not been kind to the old wooden frame which had swollen and solidified into place. After a minute of fruitless pushing, Maxine stood back and took in her surroundings again.

In the dusty space under the sink was an old-fashioned, wooden-handled toilet brush. Maxine set her mouth in a thin line and reached into the spider web that surrounded it. It felt as weighty in her hand as an axe handle. Turning her face away, she smashed the handle into the window pane. The resulting crash surely must have been heard by the men at the pump. She didn't have much time. She picked away the jagged pieces of glass, swung one leg over the sill and then the other. With a soft "oof" and a ripping of fabric, she landed in the weeds outside the window.

She got to her feet and hurried as fast as she was able toward the woods behind the gas station. The trail of crushed weeds she left behind her was easily discernible, but it couldn't be helped. Her instinct was to run, and she ran.

~*~

Mrs. Entwhistle rubbed Delilah's back. The girl was groaning now in time with the waves of internal pressure that ebbed and flowed. Checking her watch, Mrs. Entwhistle timed the pains. Every four minutes. Apparently, the poor thing had been in labor all day but hadn't realized it. Mrs. Entwhistle had had back labor with both of her deliveries. She never could understand why people said you forgot the pain. To paraphrase certain Civil War die-hards, "Fergit, hell."

"Delilah, do you have any preparations made in case you have this baby right here?"

"Nooooo! Jeff said he'd take me to the hospital."

"Just in case Jeff doesn't make it back in time, let's get some things ready, all right?"

Between pains, Delilah showed Mrs. Entwhistle where the clean towels were, and helped as best she could to make up the bed in the corner of the room with fresh linens and many layers of towels.

"Now, do you have a sharp scissors?"

"What for?" Delilah's voice was panicky.

"To cut the umbilical cord," Mrs. Entwhistle said. It was a shame, but this poor ignorant girl was going to have to grow up fast. "And I'll need boiling water to sterilize things and some new shoestrings to tie off the cord."

"I don't have new shoestrings." Delilah's wail sounded like not having new shoestrings was the end of the world.

"Then we'll just boil some old ones. Here, take them out of your sneakers."

"I want Jeff!" Delilah was crying now.

"Me, too," Mrs. Entwhistle said, "but, honey, we women have been helping each other give birth since life began. We can do this if we have to. Maybe, with some luck, Jeff will get back and take you to the hospital in time. But we'll be prepared with Plan B."

She wished she felt as confident as she hoped she sounded. Yes, she'd given birth twice, and had been present at her grandchildrens' births, but she'd never delivered a baby herself. Her mind raced over the miscellaneous information gleaned in a life time. Boil water, cut the cord, deliver the afterbirth. She began to feel an uncomfortable edge of panic. She knew most babies just pop out and start breathing, but if this one didn't, if there were complications, she had no idea what to do.

It was a long day. The hours crept. Delilah's pains were in the front now, coming strong and hard every three minutes. Exhausted, she dozed between contractions. Mrs. Entwhistle was glad for whatever respite the poor child had and sometimes nodded off herself. But then Delilah's scream would jolt both of them awake. She'd grab Mrs. Entwhistle's hand, and together they'd pant and count, surfing through a wave of pain.

Mrs. Entwhistle told Delilah not to worry, that babies take their own sweet time, but always get born eventually. She didn't know how long Delilah had been in labor without realizing it, but knew that eighteen hours for a first baby wouldn't be unusual. She didn't say that. She talked to Delilah in a calm voice, coaching, entertaining and distracting as best she could.

"How old are you, honey?"

"Six--I mean, eighteen."

"And how old is Jeff?"

"He's...older'n me. Quite a bit."

"Do your folks know about him?"

"Yeah, they hate him. That's why we had to leave, and come here when... when we had to get away. Jeff said nobody would find us out here."

"Well, it's a good thing I found you. Life is strange sometimes."

Suddenly, everything seemed to happen at once. Delilah's water broke, and headlights swept through the window. It seemed Jeff and his baby were arriving simultaneously.

Births and Rebirths

Maxine stumbled through the woods in a crouching run. Frequent glances over her shoulder revealed no Downy in pursuit. No Ridley, either. Finally, completely out of breath, she stopped and bent over gasping, hands on her knees. The woods were quiet. All she heard was birdsong. She doubted either of the men could navigate the brambles and thickets in total silence. Was no one coming after her?

Her initial feeling of relief was quickly replaced by another. What was she going to do out here in the woods by herself?

Carefully, slowly, she retraced her steps until she could see the gas station. She saw Ridley, but there was no big black car at the pump. Downy had driven off without her. Well, it made sense. Why chase down someone who was only a liability? Better to put some distance between them as fast as possible. He had the car, her purse and Cora's purse, so he had some cash and their credit cards. She didn't know why he'd taken her along in the first place, but now it seemed he'd left her behind just as he'd left Cora. A couple of tears streaked down her cheeks when she thought of her friend standing barefoot on that deserted stretch of road. How scared she must be! But then she remembered it was hard to scare Cora Entwhistle, and her own spine strengthened.

She walked out of the woods to where Ridley stood. "I'm in trouble," she said. "I need your help."

The old man looked her over from head to toe. Maxine knew she was a mess after her terrifying ride with Downy, being socked in the face twice, climbing through a broken window, and making a dash through the woods.

"Well, now," Ridley said, shifting the toothpick in his mouth from one side to the other. "I believe you broke the window in my bathroom, ain't that right?"

"Yes, I did, and I'm sorry, but it was an emergency. I had to escape from the man I was with. He kidnapped me and left my friend beside a deserted road, and now he's stolen my car. I need to call the police."

"Oh, now, I don't know that I want the police sniffin' around my place," Mr. Ridley said.

"Just let me use your phone, and I'll meet them down the road so the police don't have to come here."

"Don't you reckon they'd figure out where the call came from? I'm the only place around for miles. No, I don't think we want to be doin' that. I b'lieve you have to pay for the damage you done first, anyways."

"I will, I'll pay gladly, but Downy stole my money. You'll have to trust me for it. I really need to notify the police so they can look for my friend. She's alone out in the middle of Texas, and I'm so afraid for her."

Ridley digested that slowly. "I guess we'll take one thing at a time. The first thing is you pay for my window."

"But Downy took my purse with all my money and credit cards..." Here Maxine paused, remembering the fifty-dollar bill she'd safety-pinned in her bra. "Because you never know," she'd said to Mrs. Entwhistle. "It's not good to have all your travel money in one place."

"Excuse me," she said to Ridley. "I need to revisit

your restroom."

"Don't be runnin' into the woods again 'cause I'll come after you," Ridley said, his eyes narrowing as he suspected trickery.

"No, no more running."

When Maxine emerged, she held the fifty-dollar bill in her hand. "This should cover it and then some," she said, handing the still-warm money to Ridley.

"I reckon," he said, depositing the money in one of his capacious overall pockets.

"All of it?" Maxine raised her eyebrows. "No change?"

"Nope. You're lucky I don't report you for vandalism."

"I wish you would," she said tartly. "At least that might bring the police out here. Now I must use your phone."

~*~

"Don't push yet," Mrs. Entwhistle told Delilah. "Pant, like I showed you. We need to slow things down a bit."

"But Jeff's here now, isn't he? I saw the headlights.

He'll take me to the hospital."

"Honey, it's too late to take you anywhere. This baby is going to be born in a few minutes."

"Oh, no! What if something's wrong?"

"Don't you worry, babies know how to get born. This one will be just fine." *I hope and pray,* she added to herself.

The door opened, and a small middle-aged man backed into the room carrying a large box packed with groceries.

"Honey, I'm home," he called, still not having looked at the tableau in the room.

"Jeff!" Delilah screamed as the next contraction hit.

He whirled around and saw a stranger standing over Delilah, who lay on the bed with her back arched in pain. Hastily dumping the groceries on the table, he crossed the little room in three strides.

"Delilah, is it the baby? Who is this person? Are you all right?" He bent over the girl, tenderly wiping her damp hair out of her eyes.

"I'm Cora Entwhistle. There's no time for talk right now. We're about to have a baby."

"I'll get the truck."

"No time for that. Just hold her hand, and talk to her."

"You mean the baby's coming right here and now?"

"Right here and now. Get ready."

Delilah was pushing, and Mrs. Entwhistle could see the top of the baby's head. She positioned her hands to catch it. "Again, Delilah," she said, "push like that again. He's almost here."

With a gush of blood and fluids, the baby slid into Mrs. Entwhistle's hands. For an instant, he was silent, his eyes gazing into hers. Mrs. Entwhistle thought he trailed remnants of another world behind him like a comet's tail. She rubbed his chest gently and was rewarded by an outraged cry. He waved his fists and kicked his legs, angry at being expelled from his warm berth into a cold, bright world.

She reached for the sterilized scissors and cut the umbilical cord. Just behind her, she heard a thud as Jeff hit the floor, but she didn't have time to tend to a fainting father. Grabbing one of the warm towels at the foot of the bed, she enveloped the baby in a comforting papoose wrap that reduced his wails to whimpers. She placed him on Delilah's chest.

“Here’s your baby, honey. Here’s your little boy.”

But Delilah turned her face away. “Get him off me,” she said.

Reunited

Maxine marched into the filthy front room of Ridley's Filling Station, locked the door behind her and located an oil-stained wall phone with an old-fashioned circular dial. She dialed 9-1-1. Nothing. How far out in the sticks was she? She dialed 0 and was rewarded by a voice.

"Operator."

"Operator, I need the police. I've been kidnapped, and my car has been stolen."

"Oh my goodness! Where you at?"

"A place called Ridley's Filling Station, but I don't know what road it's on."

"I know exactly where Ridley's is. I'm gonna send the sheriff out there right now. His office is just across the street, and I can see the squad car, so I know he's there. He'll be out directly. You keep away from old man Ridley, honey, he isn't much better'n a kidnapper himself."

Maxine heard Ridley rattling the door. "Hurry, please hurry," she said. "My friend needs help, too."

"Is your friend there with you?"

"No, I don't know where she is." Maxine couldn't help it, the tears came. "Downy--the man who kidnapped me--left her beside the road somewhere. We're just passing through; we aren't from around here, and we don't know where anything is, including ourselves."

"All right, honey, now don't cry. We'll get it all sorted out. Do you want to stay on the line until the sheriff gets there?

Ridley was pounding on the door now. "Open this here door!" he yelled. "You open this door or I'll, I'll--You'll pay for this!"

"Yes, please," Maxine said to the operator. "If you'll just talk to me until help comes, I won't be so scared."

They talked while Ridley beat on the door and hollered. Maxine told the operator about how she and Mrs. Entwhistle had set out on Route 66, how they'd seen the Cadillac Ranch and the Blue Whale, about the little kitten named Marty who'd had to stay behind with the vet, about refusing to give Downy a ride, and how he'd put a nail in their tire and then hijacked them.

"Why, honey, it's like a made-for-TV movie."

"What's your name? I can't keep calling you Operator. You feel like my friend."

"My name's Polly, and I've been running this switchboard here in Jamerson, Texas, since I was a girl. I know everybody, and everybody knows me. Now you and I know each other, so that's a new friend for the both of us."

Maxine heard a siren in the distance, and apparently Ridley did, too. He stopped pounding on the door and fell silent. She peeked through the cloudy window, saw him pull a snaggle-toothed comb from his pocket and run it through his hair. He straightened his overalls and tucked in his shirt. Maxine figured he was trying to look more like a business man and less like a felon.

"The sheriff's here," she told Polly. "I can't ever

thank you enough for your help."

"You're welcome, honey. You go talk to Sheriff Martinez now. Bye-bye."

Maxine saw the black and white squad car pull into Ridley's station. Out stepped a lawman straight from Central Casting--polished boots, shining badge, holstered service revolver and level, no-nonsense gaze. Maxine suddenly felt maybe everything would be all right, after all.

"What you got, Ridley? There a lady here who needs help?"

"Yessir, Sheriff Martinez. I've got her safe in the office," Ridley said in an entirely new voice, pointing at the door. "She's all locked in, safe as can be."

Maxine twisted the lock and opened the door. "Sheriff, I'm so glad to see you. You've got to help me find my friend."

~*~

Mrs. Entwhistle heard the baby's father pick himself up off the floor. A quick glance over her shoulder showed he was shaky and white as rice pudding, but she was too busy dealing with the afterbirth to worry about him. She jerked her head toward the mother and baby on the bed.

"You better come talk to her," she said, "and see your son."

"Delilah, honey, are you okay?" he asked, tiptoeing to the bed where the girl lay with her eyes tightly closed.

The baby was still lying across her chest, but she wouldn't look at him or put her arms around him. "Take him away," she muttered, moving so violently that Mrs. Entwhistle grabbed the little boy and deposited him on the bed in a safer place. Jeff didn't spare his son as much as a glance.

Mrs. Entwhistle finished making Delilah as comfortable as she could and only then turned to Jeff. She saw he was far too old to be Delilah's husband and the father of her child. What had Delilah said when she'd asked her age? "Six--eighteen." Mrs. Entwhistle understood in an instant why this odd couple was hiding out in a remote cabin in the Texas desert. When they appeared at the hospital with a newborn infant, some sharp-eyed nurse was sure to arrive at the same conclusion and call the authorities.

"I'll get the truck, shall I? Take her—them—to the hospital?" Jeff appealed to Mrs. Entwhistle. He seemed to be at a loss about what to do next.

"Not yet, I don't think," she said. "She's exhausted. Let's let her rest an hour."

She instinctively felt that moving and jostling the new mother wasn't the best thing to do. The baby seemed to be fine. He'd fallen asleep wrapped snugly in the towel. Mrs. Entwhistle looked around for diapers, but there didn't seem to be any. Well, no matter. The towel was absorbent.

"I'm Cora Entwhistle," she said to the new father. "And you must be Jeff."

His eyes slid away from hers. "Yeah, that's right." He didn't volunteer his last name.

"Well, Jeff, congratulations on your new son. Did you and Delilah get in any baby clothes and diapers?"

"No, we were going to, but we hadn't gotten around to it yet."

"Well, that can all be sorted out soon enough. Babies don't need much. I bet Delilah's mama and daddy will be mighty glad to hear their daughter and brand-new grandson are all right."

"Yeah, well, I can call… I guess when we get to the hospital I'll call them."

"Where are y'all from?"

"We're from, uh, not around here. We only moved here recently," Jeff said, looking down at his feet.

"So you don't know too many people yet, I guess."

"No, we don't know anyone, really."

"Where do you work, Jeff?"

"I'm between jobs right now. I'm--I used to teach. High school."

Mrs. Entwhistle pressed on relentlessly. "Is that where you met Delilah? Was she one of your students?"

Jeff's anguished eyes met Mrs. Entwhistle's. "Look, I didn't mean for this to happen. I never did anything like this before. She was just so… I fell in love. I never had been in love, and she loved me, too. We couldn't stay apart."

"You were her teacher. You were in a position of trust."

"I know. It was wrong." Jeff spoke to the floor. "But when she said she thought she was pregnant, I did the right thing by her. I took her away, and we came here. We'll get married, and I'll take care of her. I promised I would."

"You could go to jail for statutory rape, Jeff." Mrs.

Entwhistle hated to say it, but she felt it had to be said. This man must face reality. "How will you take care of her then? You need to take Delilah and her baby home to her folks."

Prehensile Grip

Maxine gave Sheriff Martinez a detailed description of her car and of Mrs. Entwhistle. He shook his head and exhaled through his teeth when she got to the part about leaving Mrs. Entwhistle alone and barefoot on a dark country road.

"And the thing is," Maxine continued, "I have no idea where we were. We got our flat tire somewhere on Route 66 after we'd been in Amarillo. We were heading to New Mexico, next stop Tucumcari, but when Downy car-jacked us he turned off Route 66 and drove all over the place before he made Cora get out of the car."

"Would you say this Mrs. Ernthistle is a strong

person?" Sheriff Martinez asked.

Maxine had to smile. "It's Entwhistle, and yes, she's strong, the strongest personality I've ever known. But she's also seventy-nine years of age. No matter how strong-willed and resourceful a person may be, age has a way of catching up."

"I'll issue an All-Points Bulletin, and then I'll go looking for her myself."

"Oh, and something I didn't mention: my car is riding on one of those skinny spare tires. The man at the tire store told me I could drive on it for about fifty miles if I went slow, but Downy wasn't going slow."

"Hmm. Our friend Downy may be closer than he'd like to be. Why don't you hop in the car, and we'll take a little drive."

"But the most important thing is finding Cora," Maxine said.

"And the quickest way to do that is to get Downy to tell us where he left her."

Maxine knew he was right. She got into the passenger's seat of the squad car, rolled down the window and spoke to Ridley.

"Thank you for helping me get away from Downy,

Mr. Ridley. If you hadn't spoken up, he wouldn't have let me go to the ladies room. I'm sorry about the window, but I think the fifty dollars I gave you should be enough to fix it."

At the mention of money, Sheriff Martinez's head jerked up sharply. He looked at Ridley, who found something fascinating on the horizon. Then he walked over and silently held out his hand. Ridley shifted and shuffled, but the sheriff stood there solidly, as if he had nothing but time. Finally, Ridley reached into his pocket, withdrew Maxine's fifty-dollar bill and handed it over. Sheriff Martinez walked back to the car and passed it to Maxine. Not a word was spoken during this exchange.

Driving along the highway, their eyes scanned the road ahead for Maxine's car. "Look for a man on foot," Sheriff Martinez said. "He might not stick to the road, so look out a ways."

Maxine did. Her eyes were still sharp and made sharper by worry for Mrs. Entwhistle. It wasn't long before they came upon the Lincoln, forlorn and lop-sided on a shredded spare tire. Maxine's gaze swept the surrounding fields and spotted movement.

"There! Look to the right in the field."

The land was flat as a dinner plate and even walking

a hundred feet off the highway didn't provide cover. Downy broke into a lope when he saw them, but there was no place to go. He came to a shuffling stop and waited passively for the sheriff to approach him. Led back to the car with his hands cuffed behind his back, he subsided into the back seat with a grunt.

"Might'a known you two old bats would be more trouble'n you're worth," he said to Maxine.

"You mind your mouth," Sheriff Martinez said. "This lady will be testifying at your trial, so you might want to be nice to her. Right now you're facing car-jacking, kidnapping, assault, and elder abuse charges. Probably a lot more. I'm not a district attorney, but we've got a real good one. She'll come up a whole list of charges to put you in prison for a long time. It might go easier for you if you tell us where you left her friend. You wouldn't want to add murder to that list, would you?"

Maxine bit her lip hard, making it bleed again. She wouldn't allow herself to think anything bad might have happened to Mrs. Entwhistle, but the word *murder* clanged around in her brain like a huge bell. It didn't help that darkness was falling for the second time since her friend was left behind. Everything seemed worse at night.

~*~

Mrs. Entwhistle felt an unfamiliar and unwelcome weakness in her legs, and arms. "I'm just tired, that's all," she thought. "I walked a long way, I'm worried about Max and then all this. I'm just tired."

She gazed at the mother and baby on the bed before her. Delilah refused to open her eyes and still hadn't even looked at her baby. Jeff was sitting in a corner with his head in his hands. The baby slept like a tiny cherub, but he was bound to wake soon. He needed to be nursed and held by his mother; she knew that much. Delilah, overwhelmed by birth and hormones, had reverted to her sixteen-year-old self. She'd simply checked out. Mrs. Entwhistle thought it was time to get mother and baby moving.

"I think we can get these two to the hospital now," she said to Jeff.

He obediently rose. "I'll just pull the truck up to the door."

She heard the truck's motor start. It accelerated longer than it should have taken to approach the cabin's door. Jumping up, she ran to the window in time to see tail lights disappearing down the road. Jeff had made a new plan while he was sitting in that corner, and it didn't involve his little family. She cursed herself for having planted the idea of going to jail front and center in his head. He was gone, and she was as marooned as before, only now with a newborn to keep alive.

Delilah cracked one eye, closing it quickly when she saw Mrs. Entwhistle looking at her.

"Delilah, you open your eyes right now," Mrs. Entwhistle said. Her naturally loud voice made the baby stir restlessly. "I mean it. I know you're awake."

Delilah blinked her eyes open and stared at the ceiling. She said nothing.

"You have a fine little boy," Mrs. Entwhistle said. "He needs his mama. You brought him into this world, but if you don't take care of him, he'll leave it."

Delilah's head rose from the pillow. "You mean he'll die?"

"He could, if he's not fed and nurtured."

"But I'm so tired, and it was so awful giving birth to him. It was much worse than I thought it'd be. Nobody told me it would hurt that much. Now I just want to be my old self and sleep."

"Well, you'll never be your old self, not even if you could walk away right now and never see your baby again. He'll go right on living in your heart whether you take care of him, or put him up for adoption, or let him die of neglect. No matter what, this little boy is part of you forever."

Mrs. Entwhistle picked up the towel-wrapped bundle and placed him gently on Delilah's chest. The baby stirred, waved his tiny fists and made sucking motions with his mouth. Delilah touched his hand, and his fingers closed around hers. *Good old prehensile grip,* thought Mrs. Entwhistle. *It's probably saved millions of babies.* Sure enough, Delilah smiled even as tears poured from her eyes.

"See, he knows his mama," Mrs. Entwhistle said encouragingly. She unwrapped the baby and pulled up Delilah's shirt so that mother and baby were skin-to-skin. Nobody knew to do that in her day, but she'd read it did wonders for bonding. It seemed to be working. Delilah held her boy close, and she stroked his messy little head. Mrs. Entwhistle was reminded that she hadn't washed the birth fluids off the baby yet.

"Are you holding him securely?" she asked. "I'll heat a basin of water. That boy needs a bath. By the way, what are you going to name him?"

Delilah raised eyes now lit by love. "I thought Jeff after his daddy," she said dreamily.

"Um, okay. What's your own daddy's name?"

"My Dad? He's James."

"There you go: Jimmy Jeff. Perfect name for a Southern boy. I work for a newspaper editor named Jimmy Jack."

She didn't want to tell Delilah that Jeff had decamped, not while she was making the first tentative overtures to her baby. So far, Mrs. Entwhistle didn't think she'd noticed his absence. But she was wrong about that.

"Did Jeff leave?" Delilah asked.

"Yes."

She didn't ask where he'd gone or when he'd be back, she simply nodded and turned her attention back to the baby. Mrs. Entwhistle thought it was almost like she'd expected him to leave her. Well, whatever. Mrs. Entwhistle couldn't spare the deserter a thought. She had more important things on her mind.

Don't Do the Crime if You Can't Do the Time

Sheriff Martinez followed Downy's directions on the long, dark drive to find Mrs. Entwhistle. With Maxine beside him in the front seat and Downy handcuffed in the back, he drove until the sun came up. They crossed the county line marking the edge of his jurisdiction, so he radioed ahead to the local law officers for permission to continue.

"Asking is a courtesy, but an important one," he told Maxine. "We may need their help."

They were soon joined by two local lawmen in a squad car, and both vehicles proceeded down the dusty country roads.

"These roads look familiar? You'd better not be

playing with us, boy," Sheriff Martinez said, locking eyes with Downy in the rear-view mirror. "You're in enough trouble already; best not make me any madder than I already am."

"Yessir, I know where we're at," Downy said sullenly. "Raised up in these parts. My Pa had a little ranch around here."

It had finally penetrated his brain that he was in big trouble and faced a long stretch in prison. He'd been in jail before, several times for public drunkenness, petty theft and the like, but he'd never done time in a penitentiary. He'd heard terrible stories about prison life, though, and he couldn't stop thinking about them. He felt like crying. Why had he ever thought he could pull off a car-jacking and kidnapping? He'd wanted the car, but why the hell hadn't he just left both old ladies beside the road? What was he thinking, to drag one of them along? And then he had to go and lose his temper and smack one of them around. Pa always told him his temper would be the death of him. He stole a look at the back of Maxine's head, thankful he couldn't see the fat lip and puffy eye he'd given her.

He'd been in 'way over his head crime-wise. If that head hadn't been addled by a recent snort of coke, he'd have known he could never pull off his foggy idea about demanding a ransom. Tears pressed hot behind his eyelids. He was hungry, hung-over and scared, and he had to pee. He clenched his whole body. The only thing that could make this day worse would be to cry and wet his pants in the sheriff's car.

"Turn right at the next road," he said. "Right there's where I let her out."

There was no Cora Entwhistle to be seen, so Sheriff Martinez drove on. In a couple of miles they spotted a little cabin set back off the road in the middle of a flat field.

"Is that your folks' place?" Sheriff Martinez asked.

"Used to be. Looks deserted now. I haven't been home in quite a few years," Downy said, peering through the windshield.

The cabin seemed impossibly small. How had his parents raised a brood of children in that tiny house? Of course, they only went inside to sleep. Days were spent outdoors, the children pressed into service by their father as soon as they could toddle. Downy had an eerie feeling his life had come full-circle. He was back at the home he'd been so eager to leave, the home from which he'd walked away with his mother's weeping and his father's dire predictions ringing in his ears. Those predictions had all come true. He was a loser, a criminal, an idiot. He prayed his folks had moved on. If he saw his mother and father at that moment – well, it would just kill him to come home like this in handcuffs, in custody. Their worst fears realized. His mother would sob, and his father would take off his belt and snap it expertly. Downy shivered. In his head, he heard Pa's voice: "I beat that boy like a gong, and it don't make a dang bit of difference."

A pack of dogs boiled off the porch, barking and swirling around the cars. Downy didn't recognize any of them. Sheriff Martinez cut the engine and stepped from the car.

"Shh!" He made an explosive hushing sound and the pack quieted. The bold one, the one who'd approached Mrs. Entwhistle on the road, pushed her head up to be petted. Sheriff Martinez scratched her ears absently as he surveyed the cabin. The sun hadn't been up long and there was no sign of life. He wondered if it was deserted.

"Hello!" he called. "Anybody home?"

The door opened and a tall, barefoot, elderly woman stepped out on the porch. Maxine screamed, "Cora!," and scrambled from the car. For a moment the two women hugged, rocking back and forth a little as they released the fear they'd been holding in for hours. They left it in the dust beneath their feet.

Grandma to the Rescue

Downy Drake shrank into the back seat of the patrol car, his cuffed hands behind him at a painful angle. How he wished for the teleporter ring he'd gotten in a box of Cracker Jacks when he was a kid. If only he could be anywhere but here, the subject of discussion between the sheriff and the local lawmen.

"We've had reason to know this boy since he was a young'un. No local warrants out at the moment, not that we know of. Reckon we can let you take him on back to your jail," one of them said.

"I sure appreciate that," Sheriff Martinez said dryly. "Seeing as I arrested him and all."

"We'll take over these-here ladies, then."

Mrs. Entwhistle shot a look of concern at Maxine,

who stepped forward. "Why, no offense to y'all, but I believe we'd be more comfortable with the sheriff," she said, smiling. "I know him, you see."

"Yes, ma'am, but you're in our jurisdiction now."

Sheriff Martinez looked off into space, and spoke as though he were thinking aloud. "You'd have to take formal custody of the mother and baby, get them to the hospital and find someplace for them to stay. A lot could go wrong. The baby's only a few hours old, and his mother looks underage to me. There'll be a stack of paperwork, I guess. Social services forms, medical forms, county forms, I don't know what-all. The FBI might be involved, if she was reported as kidnapped. Those Feds, they got some forms of their own! You might have to try to find the father. That'd take some man-hours and maybe some traveling. Could get expensive."

The local men exchanged uneasy glances. They were the only members of a small, rural department; they preferred to eat supper at home and sleep in their own beds. Expense money? There simply wasn't any.

One of them stepped forward. "Well, look here, now. Why don't we put Mr. Drake in one of our cells, just informal-like, and hold him for you for a day or two while you get these ladies sorted out."

Downy's head had been swiveling back and forth like that of a spectator at a tennis match. He leaned his upper body out the window of the patrol car. "Hey, you can't just dump me with these rubes. I been in their jail before and it's a hell-hole. I got my rights!"

Three pairs of law-enforcement eyes turned to him. He saw no mercy in any of them.

"Shut up, Drake! I'm gonna call your daddy and let him tan your hide. You was always a bad'un."

Downy's bravado evaporated at the mention of his father, and he subsided into his seat, resigned to being deposited here and there like a parcel with an illegible address. He made no resistance when he was hustled from one patrol car into another.

"We'll come back for the dogs," one of the local men said. "Somebody around here will feed 'em. Don't worry, we'll take good care of your prisoner."

Downy turned to look through the rear window as he was driven away. His white, sad face was the last glimpse Maxine had of him.

"Good riddance," she said, with an uncharacteristic lack of sympathy. "He deserves everything he gets."

Sheriff Martinez helped Delilah walk carefully to his

squad car. Mrs. Entwhistle carried the baby, still wrapped in a towel, and got in the back seat with Delilah. Maxine sat in front.

Once in the car Delilah started crying and couldn't stop. "They'll take Jimmy Jeff from me," she sobbed. "They'll put him in a foster home because I'm too young. Maybe they'll even put *me* in foster care. I'll lose him."

Mrs. Entwhistle tried in vain to comfort her, but finally she sat back and thought. Then she spoke.

"You're eighteen, right?"

When Delilah started to shake her head, Mrs. Entwhistle took her chin and turned her face so she could look her in the eye. "You're eighteen, right?" she repeated meaningfully.

"Ri-right," Delilah said.

"So you're considered an adult. This is your baby, and I am your grandmother."

Delilah's eyes opened wide. *"You're…* my grandmother?" she repeated.

"That's right. I'm taking you home. We were on vacation, and the baby came sooner than expected. So now you and Jimmy Jeff just need a little check-up to make sure you're both okay, and then we'll be on our way."

She could see from the angle of Sheriff Martinez' and Maxine's heads that they were taking it all in. In fact, Maxine's head swiveled around once in astonishment, but she said nothing.

"You'll need your car," Sheriff Martinez said in a neutral voice. "I'll radio instructions that it be towed to a garage for a new tire. Maxine, I'll take you there. You can come back for Mrs. Entwhistle and Delilah when it's fixed."

Maxine nodded doubtfully. Mrs. Entwhistle knew she was worried about getting lost alone in a strange place.

"You can do it, Max. Just put the hospital's address in the GPS and follow the directions back here. After you pick us up we'll figure out what to do next." She looked over at Delilah. "What we need to do is get you back to your parents."

"They won't want me back," Delilah said. "Especially with a baby."

"Oh, I think you'll be surprised. Do your parents have other grandchildren?"

"No, this one is the first."

"Then I believe I can guarantee they'll want both you

and Jimmy Jeff. They might have to give you a good talking-to, and I don't blame them. Let them get it off their chests. Then just hand them the baby. First grandchildren are magical. They heal all wounds."

"What about Jeff?" she asked.

"I can't say about him," Mrs. Entwhistle said. "We don't know where he is or what his plans are, but the only important thing right now, the thing we have to really concentrate on, is getting you and the baby to a place where you'll be safe and looked after. Put everything else to one side."

Delilah, having exhausted herself crying, leaned her head back on the seat and closed her eyes. No one spoke until they pulled up to the emergency room entrance. Sheriff Martinez got out of the car and went inside. He returned in a minute with a wheelchair-pushing nurse.

"Out you get, Grandma," he said to Mrs. Entwhistle. "And your granddaughter and great grandson, too."

He flashed a thumbs up so briefly that she almost missed it. She sent him a glance of gratitude. Maxine hugged them both, then got back into the squad car for the trip to retrieve her Lincoln.

Mrs. Entwhistle turned her attention to the business at hand. Delilah was whisked onto a gurney and taken to a treatment room, Jimmy Jeff snug beside her. The intake receptionist handed Mrs. Entwhistle a clipboard of forms and asked her to fill them out.

"I've always wanted to write fiction," she thought, taking pen in hand. She realized she didn't know Delilah's real last name, so she christened her Entwhistle. She'd have to remember to fill Delilah in on a few details such as her name and address in case anybody asked. She hoped the girl would have the sense to remain silent until they got their stories straight.

When she was finally escorted back to rejoin her two new relatives, she saw she needn't have worried. Delilah was sound asleep, and the nurse said she'd been that way the whole time, hardly stirring during the exam.

"She was exhausted, poor thing," Mrs. Entwhistle explained. "She had a long labor and hasn't slept in two nights."

"How did you happen to be in such a remote cabin when she was almost at term?" the nurse asked.

"We didn't know she was that far along. We thought we had a month to go," Mrs. Entwhistle lied smoothly. "She came with me to my old home place to see it one more time before I die." Here she breathed a tremulous sigh. "I'm just thankful she and my great-grandson are okay. They are okay, aren't they?"

"Seem to be," said a scrub-suited doctor, brushing back the curtain around Delilah's bed. "You did a good delivery job, Grandma. I'd like to keep them overnight, just to be sure."

"Oh, no, that won't be necessary," Mrs. Entwhistle said. "I'll take them straight home and look after them there. She'll have her regular doctors and her family's support system in place at home. Don't you think that would be best?"

The doctor studied the elderly woman before him. She looked in need of a good night's sleep and wore flip flops from the hospital gift shop, but she was still the epitome of respectability. Her eyes met his steadily. He nodded.

"Yes, ma'am, that does sound best."

A nurse came in carrying Jimmy Jeff, who wore a diaper, onesie, and a little cloth hat. He was wrapped papoose-style in a blanket. Placed back in the crook of his mother's arm, the baby slept peacefully. Delilah sighed and stirred, but she didn't wake up.

"If we could just wait here until my friend gets back with the car," Mrs. Entwhistle said. "She had some, uh, car trouble and is having it fixed."

"Of course. We're not very busy, so we don't need the bed. Let's just let them sleep."

Mrs. Entwhistle slept, too, sitting upright in a chair, so weary she didn't even feel the weight of her head slumping over her chest. She felt it later, but a few minutes of refreshing sleep was worth a stiff neck.

When Maxine finally returned, all the sleepers had awakened, including Jimmy Jeff, who proved his lungs were in fine working order. Delilah had a quick tutorial in breast-feeding and was pronounced a champ when the baby latched on, nursed voraciously, and subsided again into sleepy satiety.

Before they left, Mrs. Entwhistle handed over her charge card, sending a silent thank-you to the sheriff for retrieving and returning their belongings. Downy had emptied her purse of cash, but she still had her card. She hoped Delilah's parents would see fit to pay her back for the ER visit, but if they didn't, well, it was only money. The hospital produced an approved child seat as complicated as a Rubik's cube. Mrs. Entwhistle was happy there were people to install it properly in the back seat of the car, because she knew she never could have. Finally, they were ready to leave.

"First stop, Wal-Mart," Maxine sang from behind the wheel.

"Why Wal-Mart?" Delilah asked.

"That baby needs a few things like diapers, and all you have are the clothes on your back. You need at least underwear and a toothbrush. We'll pick up essentials before we get on the road."

"Where are we going, exactly?" Delilah asked.

Mrs. Entwhistle, and Maxine exchanged glances. Where, indeed?

"We'll stay in a motel tonight," Mrs. Entwhistle decided. "And tomorrow we'll figure out our destination. You be thinking about it, Delilah."

Delilah was silent. Mrs. Entwhistle had a feeling the girl had no earthly idea where her next stop should be. Presumably Jeff had some sort of post-baby plan, but he wasn't there to implement it. Again she cursed herself for mentioning prison and scaring the new father into flight. But a part of her thought he wasn't much of a man if he could seduce a young girl, his student for heaven's sake, and then leave her in such dire straits. Maybe Delilah and Jimmy Jeff were better off without him.

Maxine asked for an isolated room at the motel,

which wasn't a problem since theirs was one of only four cars in the parking lot. Isolation proved to be a wise choice, because Jimmy Jeff's cries splintered the night. Mrs. Entwhistle marveled wearily that one little person could make such a racket. *You never forget,* she thought. *If you've ever been a mother, you always respond to that newborn cry. It's in your bones.*

She and Maxine took turns walking the baby for miles over the cheap motel carpeting while Delilah slept the sleep of exhaustion. She'd prop up on the pillows, drowsily nurse the baby, then slide back down into sleep with him on her chest. Quiet would reign for a few blissful moments.

Stories of infant suffocation ran through Mrs. Entwhistle's mind. She meant to stay awake to keep an eye on Jimmy Jeff, but in spite of her best efforts, her eyes closed. In the morning she'd protest she never slept a wink, but Maxine knew better. Mrs. Entwhistle's snores filled the space emptied when Jimmy Jeff stopped crying. Maxine asked innocently if Floyd had been a heavy sleeper.

"What in the world made you think of that?" Mrs. Entwhistle asked.

"Oh, I don't know. I was just thinking that he always seemed well-rested, Floyd did."

Mrs. Entwhistle shrugged, and moved on. “I’m going to get us some breakfast, and I’ll bring it here to the room. How do you like your coffee, Delilah?”

But it seemed Delilah didn’t drink coffee. Her parents forbade it until she was eighteen. Mrs. Entwhistle thought they’d have done better forbidding a few other things. She brought a big glass of milk instead, mentally shaking her head that a child too young for coffee was now a mother herself.

When everyone was fed, clean, and dressed, Mrs. Entwhistle called what she termed a council of war. “No point in getting in the car and just riding around,” she said. “We need to figure out where you’re going, Delilah.”

Predictably, Delilah started to cry. Overwhelmed by all that had happened in the last twenty-four hours, her brain was too addled by hormones to process it. “I don’t know,” she said between choking sobs. “I don’t have any place to go. I don’t know what to do. Could I – we – maybe just come with you wherever you’re going?”

The two ladies shook their heads simultaneously. “If we took you along we could be accused of kidnapping you,” Maxine said gently. “Besides, Jimmy Jeff needs to be in a crib, not a car seat. I think you should go home to your parents."

"But they'll hate me," Delilah cried. "They'll turn me away at the door."

"They absolutely will not," Mrs. Entwhistle said. "I guarantee they've been so worried they'll welcome you home with open arms."

She wasn't at all sure this would be true, but the family would have to work out their own dynamics. She couldn't solve everything.

Homecoming

Finally, Delilah agreed to give them her parents' address, and Maxine entered it into the GPS. "Says it should take us about three hours," she said. "Do you think we should call your folks first, give them time to be mentally prepared?"

"No! What if they tell me not to come?"

"It might be best just to show up," Mrs. Entwhistle agreed. She felt pretty sure that no grandparents could resist their first grandchild no matter how mad they were at his mother.

They approached the outskirts of Amarillo with Mrs. Entwhistle at the wheel, Maxine in the front passenger seat, and Delilah and Jimmy Jeff in the back. Both mother, and baby had slept most of the way, and Maxine whispered that it was a good thing. "It won't help Delilah's first impression any to show up at the door with a tired, screaming baby."

"Oh, my," Mrs. Entwhistle said. "Look at all this." She'd been observing that the suburbs through which they were traveling were getting fancier, and fancier.

Finally, they arrived at a discreet sign that said, "Tascosa Country Club." The houses here were huge, and set on acres of perfectly manicured green lawns.

"Can this be right, do you think?" she asked Maxine. "Should we wake Delilah and ask if we're in the right place?"

"You're in the right place," came a flat voice from the back seat. "This is where my parents live. Just keep driving to the next four-way stop and turn right. Our house is the third one on the left.

Mrs. Entwhistle followed instructions and pulled up before what had to be called a mansion. She surveyed the long, winding driveway from the street. "Do you want us to wait here, Delilah? Maybe you want to have the first meeting with your folks by yourself."

"No! I mean, thanks, but no. I don't think I can face them alone. Please come with me."

Mrs. Entwhistle drove carefully along the drive to the impressive arched front door. She turned off the engine, and they sat wordlessly and listened to it tick as it cooled. There was no sign of activity at the house; not a curtain stirred to indicate anyone was watching. Delilah began crying again.

"That girl is going to dehydrate if she doesn't stop it," Mrs. Entwhistle said to Maxine. She turned to the back seat. "Come on now, pull yourself together. You don't want to be blubbering when you greet your parents."

Jimmy Jeff chose that moment to start some blubbering of his own. "If tears win any sympathy around here we've got it covered," Maxine said. "Delilah, hand me that baby. Blow your nose and dry your eyes. Here's a wipe; run it over your face and fluff your hair up a little bit. Now let's go make your parents very happy."

Together they approached the door. Delilah dug in her purse and produced a key, but then thought better of it.

"I don't have the right to just walk in like nothing happened," she said.

Maxine, and Mrs. Entwhistle nodded. They stood there for a minute while Delilah tried to work up the nerve to ring the doorbell.

"Would you do it?" she asked.

Mrs. Entwhistle stuck her finger on the little button and gave it a good, long push. They heard the ring echoing in the house. Footsteps approached and the door was opened, but it wasn't Delilah's mother. It was a maid in a formal black dress and white apron. She even wore a frilly cap on her head. "Yes?" she said.

"I'm Delilah. I--I live here," Delilah stammered. "I used to. You must be the new maid. I left home before you started working, but I remember Mother talking about hiring you."

The maid regarded them doubtfully. Mrs. Entwhistle knew they were a motley crew--two elderly, obviously weary ladies, a red-eyed, shaky teenager, and a very new baby.

"And how may I help you?" the maid asked.

"I want to see my Mom," Delilah said, sounding about six instead of sixteen.

Footsteps clicked on the marble floor of the foyer, and a beautiful woman appeared behind the maid.

"Thank you, Marisa. I'll handle this."

Mrs. Entwhistle had to make an effort not to drop her jaw. Delilah's mother was a knock-out. *There's no way she can be the mother of a sixteen-year-old. She doesn't look over thirty herself.*

"Delilah! Is that you? And... is that a baby? Where's that disgusting man who took you away? I'll have him arrested on the spot."

"Jeff's not with me anymore, Mother," Delilah said. "I'm alone, and I've got a baby now. I've come home. I don't know what else to do."

The beautiful woman appeared unmoved by Delilah's declaration. She eyed her daughter coldly. "I see. And who are you two?"

Ignoring the rudeness with which the question was asked, Maxine introduced herself and Mrs. Entwhistle.

"Why is my daughter with you?"

"It's a long story," Mrs. Entwhistle said. "Much too long to be told on the doorstep."

She was getting impatient with this haughty woman. Didn't she realize her prodigal daughter and first grandson were standing on the doorstep of her fancy house?

"Well, I'm afraid I can't invite you in. I don't know who you are, or what you're up to. For all I know, you'll be demanding money next. As for you, Delilah, I told you before you ran away with that—that—man, you were making your bed and you would have to lie in it. You can't just come waltzing back here with a baby and expect to be welcomed with open arms."

"I don't expect that, I don't, but I have nowhere else to go, and now I have Jimmy Jeff."

"What? *Jimmy Jeff*? What kind of backwoods name is that? Oh no, my girl, you aren't pawning off your little bastard on me."

Mrs. Entwhistle felt the blood rush to her head. She opened her mouth to speak, but shut it again after receiving a quick elbow in the ribs from Maxine.

Maxine put her arm around Delilah's shoulders and turned her away from the door. Clutching Delilah's arm in one hand and Mrs. Entwhistle's in the other, she escorted them firmly back to the car.

"No more talk," she said. "What was it your mother used to say, Cora? 'Least said, soonest mended.' We're talking with our feet."

Plan "B"

Maxine silently drove them out of the fancy subdivision and found a Holiday Inn Express on the highway. With a minimum of words, she booked them into a room with two queen-sized beds. Mrs. Entwhistle knew from the set of Maxine's jaw that it wasn't a good time to ask questions, but she was intrigued. It wasn't like Maxine to take charge so forcefully.

"What are we going to do now?" she finally ventured.

"We're going to rest for two days," Maxine said. "You, and I are old, Cora. I don't know about you, but I'm exhausted. Nothing good happens when a person is too tired to think clearly, and Delilah needs rest, food, and plenty of fluids."

Mrs. Entwhistle saw the strain on her friend's face. Max's beautiful white hair was drooping, and her eyes were glassy with fatigue. Mrs. Entwhistle knew she looked just as tired. She had to make an effort to pick up her feet when she walked so she wouldn't stumble. The idea of rest was seductive.

"But what about the baby? We don't have a crib or anything."

"We've got nice, clean, dresser drawers," Maxine said, pulling one out. "We'll pad one real good with the extra blanket, and J.J. will be snug as a bug."

"J.J.? That's a good compromise," Mrs. Entwhistle said. "At least until his family gets their act together."

"I'm never going back to them," Delilah interjected. She slumped on the edge of one of the beds, too tired to cry.

"Never say never," Mrs. Entwhistle said. She wondered what in the world she was going to do with a teenager and a neonate if Delilah really meant it. "For now, we'll put everything else out of our minds, and all we'll concentrate on is resting."

For two days they watched old movies, ate take-out food, and took care of the baby. J.J. was a good feeder and with his tummy full, slept well. They all slept when he did, and woke when he cried. They had some of their best times at three a.m., making tea in the complimentary coffee pot and eating brownies from the vending machine. Delilah got some color back in her cheeks, and Mrs. Entwhistle, and Maxine began to feel like themselves again.

On the morning of the third day everyone had cabin fever, and they knew it was decision time. Check-out was at noon; Mrs. Entwhistle was determined they'd be on their way by then.

"What do you plan to do now?" she asked Delilah.

One look at her face was enough to convince anyone the girl was not capable of forming plans. Mrs. Entwhistle had anticipated that.

"We have to go back to your parents' house," she said gently.

"No! I'll never go back there. Mother rejected me, and I expected that, but I won't forgive her for rejecting her first grandchild. She didn't even look at him."

"You have a point," Mrs. Entwhistle said honestly. "But Max and I can't keep taking care of you. You're under age for one thing, and we have no legal standing as your guardians. Plus, you have a newborn to care for. You need a place to live and a means of support. At sixteen, you can't provide those for yourself. Since Jeff is out of the picture, that leaves your parents."

Delilah's face wore a mulish look, but she couldn't deny the truth. "If Mother won't let me in the house, I don't know where else to go."

"Do you have any relatives who would take you in?"

"Well, there's Aunt Jean. She lives in New Mexico, though. I don't know how I'd get there even if she'd have me."

"Maybe your mother will have reconsidered after she's had some time to think it over," Mrs. Entwhistle said. "Let's give her a chance, okay?"

Once again, they drove to Delilah's parents' house. This time her mother opened the door herself. Behind her stood a tall man.

"Daddy!" Delilah cried, pushing forward to be taken into his embrace, baby and all.

Her father held her close, murmuring in her ear and stroking her hair. Delilah's shoulders relaxed, and she leaned into his chest with her eyes closed.

Finally, he held her at arm's length.

"Now who's this here? Let's see this boy, Delilah."

She pushed the blanket away from J.J.'s face. His eyes were open wide, and he gazed into his grandfather's face as if to say, "Here I am. Am I not something?"

Mrs. Entwhistle watched with satisfaction as the baby worked his magic. His grandfather's face took on the look of stunned adoration so common in grandparents. But he had his wife to contend with, and she was not so easily swayed. She spared not a glance for J.J.

"I told you, you're not pawning that baby off on me," she said. "I've got my own life to live, and I don't intend to be the on-call baby-sitter."

"Helen!"

Delilah started crying again, and J.J. joined in sympathetically. Over the noise, Mrs. Entwhistle appealed to Delilah's father. "She has no place to go," she said in her carrying voice. "We need to talk."

He stood aside and motioned them in, then led the way to a room just off the foyer. It was filled with books and comfortable chairs. A large leather-topped desk occupied a bay window that looked out over the lawn. Mrs. Entwhistle felt a stab of pure envy. What she wouldn't give for such a room! Surely a man who had a room like this in his house also had a heart.

"I'm Jim Martin," he said, shaking hands with Maxine and Mrs. Entwhistle.

Mrs. Entwhistle realized she'd never known Delilah's real last name. It certainly wasn't Entwhistle, as she'd been christened on the hospital forms. How could she have gone through one of life's most profound experiences with Delilah not even knowing her full name?

Jim Martin was talking. "Please excuse my wife. Helen is high-strung, and she's very upset about all this."

Maxine and Mrs. Entwhistle nodded politely, not feeling the need to comment. He continued. "She'll come around in time, I think. I'll work on her. The problem meanwhile is what to do with Delilah, and--is it J.J.?"

"I named him after you, Daddy. James Jeffrey. We've been calling him J.J."

"Well, I'm flattered that you'd name him after me, his first name, anyway." Jim shifted uneasily. "Mother said Jeff is no longer with you?"

"He left us. I don't know what I would have done if these two ladies hadn't helped me. Can't I come home, Daddy?" Delilah's voice had gone high, and shaky. "I could live in the pool house, and I'll take care of J.J. myself. *She* won't have to help. She won't even have to see us."

Jim Martin couldn't quite meet his daughter's eyes. "Look, I know it's a bad situation, but your mother warned you if you went away with Jeff you couldn't come home again. She feels she can't go back on her word now."

"Can't... you mean she won't. It's not just me anymore. I have a baby--your grandchild. What am I supposed to do if you won't help me?"

Jim Martin reached for his back pocket. Mrs. Entwhistle knew if he pulled out his wallet and offered them money, she'd put her fist right in the middle of his face. She vowed to herself that she wouldn't even accept reimbursement for the hospital bill from these gutless people. She took a deep breath to tell Delilah's father what she thought of parents who would fail to help their child in need, but Maxine cut in smoothly.

"Of course, you must take your time to get used to this new situation in your family," she said. "The thing is, we've only known Delilah for a few days, and we're traveling, but we can't leave without knowing that she and her baby are in a safe place."

"I suggested to Helen that maybe Delilah could stay with my sister, Jean. It would be just for a little while, you know, until things settle down." Delilah's father threw a look of appeal at Mrs. Entwhistle and Maxine.

"Daddy, I love Aunt Jean, but does she really want me right now?"

"All we can do is ask, honey." He turned to Mrs. Entwhistle and Maxine. "Helen has forbidden me to give Delilah any help. She said if Jean agrees to take her in, she and the baby can get there on the bus." Jim extracted several bills from his wallet and pressed them into Delilah's hand. "Here, I want you to have this. Don't tell your mother," he whispered.

Mrs. Entwhistle's voice dripped ice. "If you will kindly make whatever arrangements need to be made with your sister, we will take Delilah and J.J. there ourselves. With your permission, of course." This last was delivered in such a sarcastic tone that Maxine put a warning hand on Mrs. Entwhistle's arm.

Ghost Town

When Mrs. Entwhistle made her declaration--it couldn't really be called an offer--that she and Maxine would deliver Delilah to Aunt Jean, she had no idea where Jean Martin lived. Hearing she resided in a town called Glenrio which straddled the Texas/New Mexico border, Mrs. Entwhistle looked it up in her atlas. It was only a little more than an hour's drive away. Delilah's father called the motel that night to say he'd spoken to his sister, and she would be pleased to welcome Delilah and her baby. Mrs. Entwhistle put the phone on speaker.

"You may find Jean rather eccentric," Jim Martin said. "She lives in a remote area, not many other people around. She and her late husband moved to

Glenrio many years ago when it was still a town. It's pretty much deserted now. In fact, I think Jean may be the entire population. But she has a decent house, and she sounded enthusiastic about having some company."

"Aunt Jean is just plain weird," Delilah said, "but I've always loved her. *She* has a kind heart."

"This is just temporary, Dee-Dee," her father said pleadingly. "Just until I can talk Mother around. Then you and the baby can come back home where you belong."

Mrs. Entwhistle thought about that conversation as they drove through Llana Escatado, the Staked Plains. She could imagine cowboys twirling their lariats as they herded dusty longhorn steers through the barren landscape, searching for a watering hole. Tumbleweeds drifted across the road and the surrounding landscape was bleached white as a skull. What would inspire anyone to make their home in such barrenness?

"Glenrio isn't really a town anymore," Delilah said. "I guess it's more of a ghost town. I don't want you to be shocked when we get there."

Mrs. Entwhistle appreciated the warning. Glenrio was no more than a tiny collection of derelict buildings crowded close to the road. They gazed at the ruins of a post office, a diner, a gas station, and a few other buildings whose original use couldn't be determined. The buildings looked like bad teeth, stubby and forlorn.

"Wow!" Maxine said, "this is great! It could be a movie set."

"Maybe for a horror movie," Mrs. Entwhistle said.

"It actually was a movie set," Delilah said. "Aunt Jean likes to tell the story of how, back in 1938, Glenrio was used as a location for filming part of 'The Grapes of Wrath.'"

"Where does your aunt live?" Mrs. Entwhistle asked. Surely she didn't live here. None of the buildings were inhabitable.

"Go on through town and turn left at the next crossroads," Delilah said. "That will put us in New Mexico. The town straddles the border, so part of it is in Texas, part in New Mexico."

Mrs. Entwhistle did as directed and there looming ahead on the flat prairie sat a house so incongruous with its surroundings that she let the car roll to a gradual stop so she could stare. A genuine Victorian Painted Lady, resplendent in shades of mauve, gray, coral, and teal, the house stretched three stories above its sandy yard. Towers, gingerbread trim, and multi-paned windows topped a wide porch that wrapped the width of the house and disappeared around the corner in a frenzy of architectural chutzpa.

Mrs. Entwhistle eased the car down the sandy road and into the driveway. She switched off the motor, and they contemplated the unlikely scene before them in silence. Then the front door flew open and, like a cuckoo emerging from a clock, a tiny figure appeared.

"Aunt Jean, hi!" Delilah was out of the car in a flash. She ran to the porch and leaned down to hug her aunt, who could have stood erect under Delilah's outstretched arm.

Mrs. Entwhistle and Maxine exchanged a look of wonder. "Is she a midget?" Mrs. Entwhistle asked out of the side of her mouth.

"I think the correct term is little person," Maxine whispered back.

J.J. howled from his car seat behind them. It was the cry they'd learned meant, "You'd better get me out of here and feed me right NOW, or there'll be hell to pay." Delilah's head turned when she heard her baby's cry, and she hurried back to the car.

"J.J., it's time to meet your great aunt," she said, dealing with the straps and buckles to release him. "And you two come on. I want to introduce you to Aunt Jean."

Mrs. Entwhistle and Maxine got out, hobbling the first few steps after sitting for an hour. They approached the little woman who waited on the porch. She looked them up and down and apparently approved of what she saw, because she opened her arms for hugs. Mrs. Entwhistle had been preparing to offer a handshake; she wasn't big on hugs. Maxine got right into the spirit, though, and stooped to hug Aunt Jean enthusiastically.

"Well, aren't you two just exactly right!" Aunt Jean proclaimed in a voice so deep it seemed to belong to someone else. "I can't thank you enough for looking after my girl here and her baby. He's a corker, isn't he?" There wasn't a trace of judgment in her voice – nothing but delight, and pride.

Mrs. Entwhistle tried not to stare, but it was difficult. Jean wore a multi-layered pastel tutu and a leopard-print tee shirt. On her feet were miniscule pink sneakers that lit up when she walked. She could have shopped nowhere but in the children's department. Her white hair was held back by a ribbon, and her eyeglasses sparkled with sequins. Standing on the gingerbread-trimmed porch of her ornate house, she reminded Mrs. Entwhistle of a doll suddenly come to life.

“Come in, come on in. I’ve got tea ready.”

They followed their hostess into a house so accurately furnished and decorated in Victoriana it could have been a museum. On a dining room table that could have easily seated twelve, Jean had laid out a dainty tea party. There were cucumber sandwiches (no crusts), scones with whipped cream, strawberries dipped in chocolate, and a large pot of Earl Grey tea. Mrs. Entwhistle’s stomach gave an anticipatory rumble.

“You shouldn’t have gone to so much trouble, Aunt Jean,” Delilah said, preparing to nurse J.J. “You don’t mind if I nurse him here, do you?”

“Not a bit. We’re all girls together. Now, ladies--may I call you Cora and Maxine?--please sit down and help yourselves.”

Mrs. Entwhistle preferred to be called Mrs. Entwhistle, but she thought it would seem unfriendly if she said so. After all, Jean had fixed a lovely tea for them. The cucumber sandwiches were especially yummy. She ate six before she knew it. Maxine shot her a warning look and shook her head faintly.

"Well, they're small," Mrs. Entwhistle murmured in defense.

Jean's laugh was as deep and hearty as her voice. "Now don't hold back. Cucumber sandwiches don't keep, so what we don't eat will be wasted."

Light struggled to get through the elaborate velvet swags and pelmets at every window, but eventually Mrs. Entwhistle could tell day was fading. "Max, it's time for us to get back on the road. We've got a ways to go to Albuquerque before night falls."

"Nonsense!" Jean said. "It's a good three-hour drive, and I wouldn't dream of letting you start out now. It'll be dark soon and there's nothing darker than a desert highway. No indeed, you'll be my guests tonight."

Mrs. Entwhistle correctly interpreted the look Maxine sent her, and they accepted Jean's offer with thanks. They both had trouble seeing at night, and at home they only drove on streets they knew well. Neither of them relished the thought of driving off into the sunset on an unfamiliar road. Jean directed them to bring in their luggage and showed them to their room. Following their tiny hostess's energetic climb up the curving flights of stairs to the third floor, Mrs. Entwhistle was glad once again they'd decided to travel light. She was out of breath when they reached the room that was to be theirs for the night.

Located in the round tower that protruded from the roof like a lighthouse, the room had a semi-circle of windows with no Victorian draperies to obstruct the view. Unlike the rest of the house, this room was Spartan in its appointments. Two white wooden twin beds with plain white coverlets, two straight chairs, two hooks on the wall to serve as closets, and an old-fashioned wash stand with a flowered ewer and basin--that was it.

Mrs. Entwhistle felt her mind and body relax. She could breathe here. This room felt infinitely more comfortable to her than the rest of the house. She turned to thank Jean, but she'd vanished without another word. They heard her footsteps rapidly clattering down the stairs.

"Well!" Maxine said, sitting down with a bounce on one of the beds. "The beds seem okay, and isn't this room something? I feel like I'm in a ship at sea."

"A ship in the middle of an ocean of sand," Mrs. Entwhistle said, trying out her bed. "Ah, yes, I like a hard mattress. This'll do just fine. I guess we're supposed to go on to bed?"

"I guess. She left like she wasn't expecting to see us

again until morning."

"That's good, actually. I'm beat."

They felt a bit exposed getting ready for bed in a room without curtains, but after all, who was going to be peering in from the desert three stories below? Mrs. Entwhistle stood with her toothbrush in hand. "Did she mention anything about a bathroom up here?"

"I don't think so, but surely there must be one. Let's explore."

In their long white nightgowns, they crept out into the hallway and looked around. No bathroom in sight. Holding onto the banister, they carefully descended a short run of shadowy stairs to a landing with two doors opening from it. The first one was locked, but the second opened into a huge old-fashioned bathroom the likes of which they'd only seen in history books. The tub stood so tall on its claw feet they wondered how they'd ever manage to get in and out of it without falling. The toilet was topped by a large porcelain water receptacle that apparently emptied when you utilized a white knob that read "Pull."

"Oh, my," Mrs. Entwhistle said, surveying the tub doubtfully. "I think I'll skip my bath tonight."

"Yes, I will, too."

"I sure hope I don't have to get up during the night," Mrs. Entwhistle said. "Those stairs… and I didn't see a light switch."

"I'll show you how to use the flashlight in your phone," Maxine said.

Mrs. Entwhistle's stomach gave an embarrassingly loud growl. "You know, we didn't really have dinner, just those little cucumber thingies. I could eat."

"Jean didn't mention dinner. Maybe she doesn't have it herself. I think I've got a bag of M & M's in my purse," Maxine said. "We'll have a picnic in a tower and pretend to be Rapunzel."

Leave it to Max, Mrs. Entwhistle thought, to make the best out of any situation. On the landing she couldn't resist trying the locked door again. "I know I'm being nosy," she said, shaking the brass handle, "but what do you suppose is in here?"

Maxine made big eyes and fluttered her fingers. "Knock, knock," she sang, "who's there? Ghost. Ghost whooooo?"

"Brrr!" Mrs. Entwhistle hugged herself against the cold breeze that seemed to be blowing from under the door. "'From ghoulies, and ghosties, and long-legged beasties, and things that go bump in the night, Good Lord deliver us.' Come on Max, time for bed."

But before she could sleep, she had a column to write. Wearily propping herself up on a pillow, she balanced her laptop on her knees and began.

I met a person short of stature today and learned the correct term is little person. It's difficult to think how such a big heart could fit in this particular little person. She counts as one of the wonderful souls who have peopled this trip – along with some bad 'uns, too, human nature being what it is. But let me tell you about her house....

Mrs. Entwhistle's head drooped forward as her eyes closed. She never did press Send that night.

On The Road Again

They were awakened early by the unfiltered dawn. There's something to be said for curtains, Mrs. Entwhistle thought, pulling the pillow over her face and trying to go back to sleep. It was no use. Once awake she stayed awake. It was the same at home, leading to some early mornings in the kitchen with her teacup and Roger for company. Squinting, she looked at her watch and saw that it was only five thirty. Would Jean be up this early? Where was the kitchen, and would it produce coffee and breakfast? She felt an urgent need for food after skipping dinner the night before.

In the opposite bed, the mound that was Maxine stirred. An arm came out of the covers and shielded her eyes. "What time is it?" she asked thickly.

"Too darn early-o'clock," Mrs. Entwhistle answered. "The way the sun hits this room is better than a rooster. I'd buy some curtains if I lived here."

"Do we dare go downstairs this early? I'd kill for a cup of coffee."

"And bacon, eggs, and toast."

"Let's chance it."

Propelled by hunger, the ladies dressed quickly and walked stealthily down the two flights of wooden stairs, cringing at every creak. They followed a light at the end of a long hall and found themselves in an antique kitchen. It was lined with English-style dressers upon which rested more blue and white china than Mrs. Entwhistle had ever seen in one place. There was a long, pine trestle table in the middle of the room, and there sat Delilah with a cup in one hand and J.J. in the other.

"Good morning," she said, looking as fresh as only the young can look early in the morning.

"Morning," Maxine, and Mrs. Entwhistle chorused. "Coffee?"

"Help yourselves. I made a pot. I decided I'm old enough to drink it now, and I've been up since five with this little monster."

"Was he crying? We didn't hear a thing up there in our tower."

"No, he was just wide awake. I hope he isn't getting his days and nights mixed up. I've heard that can happen."

"You'll be able to get him on a decent schedule now that you're settled here with your aunt. He's been pillar-to-post ever since he was born," Maxine said.

"How long do you think you'll stay with Jean?" Mrs. Entwhistle asked.

"No idea. I guess until Daddy talks Mother into letting me come home. I don't know how long that might take. I don't even know if I want to go back."

"You have some big decisions to make," Mrs. Entwhistle said. "At your age, and with a baby to support, you don't have a lot of good options." She hated to rub it in, but Delilah sometimes showed an alarming disconnect with reality.

"This seems like a good place to catch your breath and think what to do next," Maxine said. "You'll need to figure out how to finish high school, and get established with a pediatrician for J.J.'s well-baby check-ups. This place is so remote. Does your aunt have a car?"

"She does have a car, a vintage Cadillac that still looks like new and slurps gas, but she loves it. I suppose she'll know where the nearest doctor is."

"What about finishing school?"

"High school seems like it happened to someone else." Delilah thought for a moment. "Actually, I can't imagine going back to my old life. Too much has happened; I'm a different person now. I know I'll have to at least get my high school diploma and then think about college, but I can't get my mind around it right now. Maybe I'll be able to take classes online."

Mrs. Entwhistle felt uneasy at leaving Delilah and J.J. in a place so buried in the desert, but after all, the girl's father had made the arrangements. Jean had obviously lived here for many years and surely knew her way around. The important thing was that Delilah and J.J. were safe and cared for. She had to quit fussing about the details. Diane and Tommy often accused her of having "control issues," whatever those were.

Maxine had been poking around the kitchen and came up with a frying pan and the ingredients for breakfast. "Do you think Jean would mind if I scrambled some eggs?" she asked Delilah.

"No, go ahead. Jean never gets up before noon."

"How does she keep up this big place all by herself?" Mrs. Entwhistle asked.

"Oh, she has loads of help. The maid arrives at seven, the cook comes in the middle of day to make the one meal Aunt Jean eats, and the odd-job man is here at least twice a week. He mostly paints the house. The desert air is hard on paint, and he's constantly re-painting. He never gets finished."

"Great job security for him. Say, do you know what's in that room off the third-floor landing? It's locked and there was a really cold draft coming from under the door," Mrs. Entwhistle said.

Delilah shook her head. "It's always been locked since I can remember. I asked Aunt Jean about it once, but she said it was just storage, suitcases, and trunks and things."

Maxine's scrambled eggs were appreciatively consumed, and everyone had another cup of coffee. Then Mrs. Entwhistle looked at her watch again and said, "We really should be on our way. You say Jean sleeps until noon?"

"I don't know if she sleeps that long, but she doesn't come out of her room until noon," Delilah said.

"Would it be terribly rude if we left before she emerges? We could leave her a note of thanks for her hospitality."

"I'm sure she'll understand. You've already gone miles out of your way for me, and I've delayed your trip for days. I'll never be able to thank you enough," Delilah's nose turned pink as she teared up a little.

"Now don't get upset, honey," Mrs. Entwhistle said, patting her on the shoulder. "It'll come right through in your milk, and then you'll have a fussy baby. We only did what any mother would do." She stopped, and bit her lip. She hadn't meant to take a swipe at Delilah's mother, but the girl didn't seem to notice her faux pas.

"We'll stay in touch, won't we?" Delilah asked, sounding very young.

"Of course we will," Maxine, and Mrs. Entwhistle chorused. "We'll want to see how that baby grows and know how you are doing."

"Do you know how to make video calls?" Delilah asked.

Mrs. Entwhistle shook her head no, but Maxine nodded. "I sure do, and it's a great idea. That's how we'll keep up with each other. How about if we video call each other every Sunday?"

"That would be tomorrow."

"We'll skip this week, but after that you call us when you have a spare minute. We'll tell you where we are and what we're doing. You can tell us how you're settling in, and how J.J.'s adjusting."

"Oh, and one thing, Delilah. Stay away from that locked room," Mrs. Entwhistle said, looking a little embarrassed.

"Why?"

"No reason, really. Just... so drafty, you know. You don't want to catch a cold."

~*~

"That Jean was a peculiar person, wasn't she? I mean, it was nice of her to take in Delilah and J.J. and mighty hospitable of her to have us stay the night, but don't you reckon, if it'd been you, you'd have got some food around?"

"Well, of course, but sounds like she only eats one meal a day, and maybe she just didn't think of it. People get stuck in their ways, you know."

"Did we leave her a note?" Mrs. Entwhistle asked in a sudden panic. "I can't remember writing a thank you note."

"I did," Maxine said. "And I signed both our names. You were carrying the bags downstairs when I did it."

"Phew! Good thing you've got a mind. I sure miss mine," Mrs. Entwhistle said, and they laughed ruefully.

"You have to laugh at memory lapses at our age, or else you'd think for sure you had dementia," Maxine said.

"I think that anyway," Mrs. Entwhistle said. "Remember that time I asked the doctor if he thought I had Alzheimer's? He said if a person has enough self-awareness to worry about it, they're probably okay."

"That's some comfort, I guess. But listen, Cora, you're still sharp as a tack."

"Some days I'm tark as a shack." Mrs. Entwhistle grinned and shook her head ruefully.

"I'm curious about something," Maxine said. "Why did you ask Delilah to stay away from that locked room on the third floor? Do you think it's haunted or something?"

"You know I don't believe in the supernatural, but that room just gives me the heebie-jeebies."

"That's not like you. You always say you don't do woo-woo."

"I don't. But there was something about that cold draft that made all the hair on my arms stand up. I think it's sensible to pay attention to one's intuition. Don't you?"

"Intuition. Yes, very sensible indeed." Maxine looked out the window to hide a smile.

The Sweat Lodge

Mrs. Entwhistle was behind on her dispatches to the *Pantograph*, and she felt guilty. She'd meant to send Jimmy Jack a column every day or two, but what with being kidnapped, delivering a baby, caring for a new mother, and staying in a haunted (maybe) house, she'd missed a few days. She set up her laptop and got to work. She found herself in the dilemma of many diarists: when she had time to write, it was because nothing much was going on. When events escalated, there wasn't time to record them.

We've seen *a lot more of Texas than we'd planned on seeing and met some of the best and worst people on the planet,* she began, but there she stopped. How could she condense the events of the last few days into eight hundred words? And how much could she even reveal without compromising her testimony in Downy's upcoming court case? She was stumped. Maybe if she called home, it would clear her mind. Dex answered on the first ring.

"Mrs. E! I was getting worried. You didn't answer any of my calls or texts."

"I know, Dex, I'm sorry, but we were in an area where the cell coverage was iffy. How's everything at home? How's Roger? How are you? I'm going to put you on speaker so Maxine can hear, too."

"Okay. Hi, Maxine."

"Hi, sweet boy."

"Let's see. First, everything is good here. Booger brought a load of mulch for your flower beds and spread it himself. He wouldn't let me help. He said he owes you so much he can never repay you. I think he's still sweet on you, Mrs. E."

"Now stop that, Dex. Booger's an old rascal, that's all. He look okay?"

"Yes, he looked fine. I think he's lost weight--his overalls were hanging on him."

"Well, good, he needed to after that heart attack. How's Roger?"

"Roger sleeps twenty hours out of twenty-four. The other four hours he eats and pees. Does that sound about right?"

"Yes, that's Roger. Does he miss me, do you think?"

"He didn't eat the first two days, but after that he seemed to accept the situation. He sits beside me while I study. Oh, and he's had a few accidents in the house."

"He's old; that happens. Just clean it up as best you can, and I'll deal with stains and such when I get home. Poor old pup, he can't help it. Now tell me about you. How's your online course work coming?"

"Actually, pretty well. I find that method of learning suits me."

"And have you heard from Lara?"

"No. That's over."

"Are you okay with it?"

"I have to be, don't I?"

Mrs. Entwhistle and Maxine exchanged meaningful looks, shook their heads and pursed their lips. They hated to think of Dex enduring heartbreak, but they knew it was an inevitable part of growing up.

"What about Jimmy Jack? He say anything about not getting my columns the last few days?"

"I saw him at the Busy Bee Diner yesterday, and he asked if I'd heard from you. He was concerned if you were all right. I'll run over after we hang up and tell him I've talked to you.

"Tell him I'm sending him two columns today," Mrs. Entwhistle promised recklessly. "Now I'll let you get back to your studies."

Mrs. Entwhistle was quiet for a long time after that. Maxine glanced over from time to time, but didn't say anything. She knew when to leave her old friend alone with her thoughts.

Finally, Mrs. Entwhistle turned back to her computer and resumed typing. *A Texas sheriff named Martinez, a badlands bandit named Downy Drake, a very young mother, and a brand-new baby have made the last few days memorable. We're driving along Route 66 trying to ignore the coyote heads stuck on fence posts and taking in the desert landscape. It has its own beauty, very different from the green, green grass of home. The sunsets make up for the daytime dust, and at night the stars look like sequins sewn on velvet.*

Here are some things Maxine, and I have learned so

far: pack for a road trip with the thought that you might have to take everything out of the trunk to get at your spare tire. Be ready to join in whatever the natives have going, be it food or activities. Whether it's viewing a blue whale or eating saag paneer at a roadside motel, be open to new experiences. You'll meet some lovely people and a few you'd rather do without. But isn't that a lot like home?

~*~

Maxine was reading from her guide book as they approached Albuquerque. "Looks like we're coming up on the Sandia Mountains. Says here there's a tram that goes to the top--almost two miles high. What do you think?"

Mrs. Entwhistle considered it. Maxine continued: "You can see 11,000 square miles. Let's see, there's a Visitors Center, restaurant, and hiking trails. Well, we sure don't want to hike."

"No, we sure don't."

"And it says wear layers; it's cold up there."

"Our sweaters are in the back," Mrs. Entwhistle said. "Let's take a look, and then we'll decide if we want to do it."

They drove into the parking lot, parked, and

approached the ticket kiosk. Looking up, they saw a glass-sided tram gliding up as another glided down on parallel overhead cables. The cables hummed eerily in the wind, and the carriages bounced a bit.

“You want tickets?” the man in the kiosk asked. “Trams may not be running much longer--getting too windy. Those gondolas really rock and roll when the wind kicks up.”

People were disembarking. Some were talking about the ride and the sights they’d seen. Some were quiet and looked a bit shaky. A woman had one hand over her mouth and the other clutching her stomach. Mrs. Entwhistle and Maxine turned without a word and headed back to their cars. Some things didn’t need discussion.

They drove on in brilliant sunshine, so bright it made them both sleepy. Mrs. Entwhistle sat up straight and opened her eyes wide, fighting to stay awake. She was driving; it wouldn’t do to doze off. She looked around alertly. On her left she saw a small, hand-painted sign:

Sweat Lodge
Sunset Ceremony
All Welcome
Two Miles

“Max, did you see that sign for a sweat lodge?” Mrs.

Entwhistle said. "What do you think that's about?"

"I've read about those ceremonies. You sit in a kind of lean-to and they pour water on hot rocks to make steam. You sweat, and it's supposed to be purifying. Some people see visions and such. I've always wanted to try it."

"You have? Well, you'll never get a better chance. Want to stop and see about it?"

"We'd want to be sure it's an authentic Native American ceremony. People have died in bogus sweat lodges," Maxine said. "That's what I've read, anyway."

Mrs. Entwhistle bumped the big car down a one-lane dirt road for what seemed like a long way. They came upon a scattering of adobe houses. One of the houses had a similar hand-painted sign: *Sweat Lodge Here*. She stopped the car, and she and Maxine got out. They stood looking at the house, working up the nerve to knock, when an Indian woman emerged.

"Hello," she said. "Welcome. Have you come for the sweat lodge ceremony?"

"Maybe," Mrs. Entwhistle said. "We'd like to know more about it, anyway."

"Come in, please; come into my home."

The woman smiled then, her wrinkled brown face illuminated by a smile so warm they forgot any misgivings about entering a stranger's house in the middle of the desert. "Thank you," they chorused and followed her across the threshold.

It was noticeably more comfortable inside; the thick adobe walls retained the night's coolness. Bright woven blankets covered the furniture, and painted pots spilled over with profusions of healthy greenery. Mrs. Entwhistle saw Maxine's eyes light up. It was exactly the kind of place she liked.

Their hostess motioned for them to have a seat. "My name is Anna Flying Fox, and I am of the Pueblo people. What is your interest in the sweat lodge ceremony?"

"Well, we're curious, I guess," Maxine said. "I've read a bit about Native American culture and about the sweat ceremonies. It just seems like a missed opportunity if we are right here and don't participate in one, but I've heard it can be pretty rigorous. Are we too old?"

Anna beamed her wonderful smile at them again. "It is my responsibility and my privilege to tailor the ceremony to the needs of the participants. You are the age of wisdom, as am I. Do you bring a special intention for healing?"

"No," Maxine began, looking apprehensively at Mrs. Entwhistle. She knew her friend didn't have much patience with what she called "woo-woo." But Mrs. Entwhistle spoke up.

"Yes," she said. "I have an intention."

Maxine looked at her in surprise.

"Not for myself," Mrs. Entwhistle added.

"And you?" Anna Flying Fox looked at Maxine.

"I'm open to whatever happens."

Anna nodded. "Then we will proceed. It is nearly sunset, and that is the best time for the ceremony. My grandsons will stoke the fire under the rocks and bring pails of water. I suggest you wear something loose and cool."

"We're limited to what's in our suitcases," Mrs. Entwhistle said. "We do have nightgowns. Will there be anyone else in there with us?"

"No one else will be there, only the two of you and me. Nightgowns will be just fine. Now I will bring you water to drink while we prepare. It's important to be as hydrated as possible before we begin."

An hour later Mrs. Entwhistle and Maxine, dressed in their long white nightgowns, followed Anna to a small adobe dome. They had to stoop to enter through the low doorway. Inside were rough benches in a semi-circle around a pit. In the pit were large, red-hot rocks. Sweetgrass and cedar branches released their fragrance into the air. Anna seated them and began a prayer in her native language. When she finished, she reached for the pail of cool water at her side and poured it carefully over the rocks.

Instantly a dense steam rose. Mrs. Entwhistle was reminded of when Diane and Tommy were little and had croup. She'd take them into the bathroom, turn on the hot water and make a tent of towels over their heads. She took a deep breath, feeling the steam clear her lungs. The first beads of sweat prickled her scalp.

"Now you will think of your intention and talk to the Great Spirit," Anna said, pouring another pail of water over the rocks.

Mrs. Entwhistle obediently closed her eyes and turned her thoughts inward. She felt steam and heat, and heard Anna's guttural chanting. Her mind emptied of Downy Drake, Delilah, and all the strange, wonderful, frightening things that had happened to her since she began her trip on Route 66. Images came and went. She saw Floyd so clearly she reached out to touch him; then she saw her parents, dead these thirty years. It bothered her that her loved ones seemed not to notice her, but she let the feeling go, and it floated away. Whatever happened was the way it should be. She leaned her head back against the wall, breathed in the steam and stopped hearing the water splash on the rocks. Time ceased to matter. There was only heat and a wide, restful emptiness in her mind.

Anna's hand on her shoulder brought Mrs. Entwhistle back to herself. "Is it over?" she asked, her voice emerging as a croak.

"If it is over for you," Anna said.

Maxine was struggling to her feet, her long white gown as wet as if it had been dipped in water. "It is for me. I've had enough," she said, heading for the door unsteadily. "Thank you," she added over her shoulder. Maxine wouldn't forget her manners in hell.

Anna hurried to put a hand under Maxine's arm and escort her out. Mrs. Entwhistle sat dreamily, reluctant to summon the energy to get up. She became aware that her hair was plastered to her head and her own gown was clinging to her in a most unladylike way. Gradually, these things mattered again. She rose carefully and made her way to the door, keeping one hand on the wall for balance. It was completely dark. Where had the time gone?

"I'm not sure what to do," she confessed to Anna. "I didn't think about it being so dark when we finished. Are we far from a motel where we can spend the night?" She wasn't at all sure she was safe to drive.

"You are both welcome to stay with me tonight. I have two extra beds."

Ordinarily, neither Maxine nor Mrs. Entwhistle would have dreamed of taking up a stranger's offer to spend the night, but somehow Anna Flying Fox didn't seem like a stranger. They followed her into her house, got into dry clothes, fell into bed and slept. Not one thought of a column disturbed Mrs. Entwhistle's slumber.

Standin' on the Corner

"So what was your intention?" Maxine asked as they drove away from Anna Flying Fox's house the next morning. "You don't have to tell me if you don't want to."

"I won't, Max, if you don't mind. I'll tell you if it comes true, though."

"Of course, I don't mind. I'm not sure it's like wishing on a star, though."

"Time will tell, and if it does, *I'll* tell."

"Interesting that I was the one who wanted to go through a sweat ceremony, but you were the one who got the most out of it. I was mostly just itchy and sweaty, and I got the worst headache from the heat."

"Well, you never know what life will bring," Mrs. Entwhistle said philosophically.

She had her laptop out and was trying to find a way to describe the sweat ceremony to the readers of the *Pantograph.* It was tricky, because if she looked at the screen for more than a minute at a time, she felt carsick. Laboriously, she typed between steadying glances at the horizon.

It was a little like a really good massage, a little like a Baptist Church altar call, and a little like a ghost story told around the camp fire. I didn't expect to be so immersed in the proceedings, planning beforehand to keep a reportorial eye open so I could give you an objective account. Instead, as it got hotter and hotter, and steamier and steamier, I fell into kind of a trance in which I saw visions that seemed real--so real I stretched out my hand to touch my late husband. You readers who play video games and are familiar with virtual reality will know what I mean. It wasn't scary, and I never felt threatened. Our leader maintained a calm demeanor, and I felt safe with her. Would I do it again? Probably not, but I'm glad I had the opportunity to do it this once. Incidentally, I think I also lost a few pounds.

She read what she'd written to Maxine. "Too bad we don't have a scale."

"I know, but I can tell I'm thinner by the way my clothes feel," Maxine said. "If we got nothing else out of it, we sweated off a bit of weight."

"It will probably come back with the next good meal. Okay, what's our next stop?"

"The Petrified Forest," Maxine said. "Look it up, why don't you, and read it to me. What are we going to see?"

"Let's see... the Painted Desert is part of the Petrified Forest--no, other way around. The region is famous for its rocks containing bands of colors. Looks like we can drive through part of it by staying on Route 66. Oh, listen to this: Newspaper Rock contains 650 petroglyphs that are two thousand years old."

As they approached Arizona, the roadside attractions grew tackier. Concrete teepees squatted beside garishly-painted trading posts, blocking the view of stunning red mesas. Gift shops shouted their wares.

"Gift shops are the same everywhere," Maxine said. "Do you want to stop at any of 'em?"

"Nope. Well, there is one in the guidebook that looks

interesting--Stewart's Petrified Wood Trading Post. You can legally buy petrified wood there, and it's right on our way."

"Do you actually want petrified wood?"

"No, I promised myself I wouldn't bring one more thing into my house unless I took two other things out. But I'd like to see the wood close up."

"Well, it says here to look for green dinosaurs."

When the green dinosaurs showed up in the distance, Mrs. Entwhistle and Maxine were ready. "That's got to be the trading post. Says here they have dinosaurs eating mannequins. Oh, and ostriches. You can feed the ostriches; I guess the dinosaurs are full after eating all the mannequins."

Maxine pulled into the parking lot, and they ventured into the blazing sun of noon. There seemed to be a crowd, judging by the cars outside, but the trading post itself was all but empty.

"Where is everyone?" Maxine asked the clerk at the cash register.

"Oh, you mean the cars? The owner bought a bunch of junkers and had them hauled here to make it look like we're doing a booming business. People are more apt to stop if they see a full lot."

They made a quick tour of the merchandise, spending a few minutes marveling at the colors in the petrified wood on sale, but neither made a purchase. As they left, the sales clerk suggested they buy plastic bags of ostrich food to feed the birds on their way out. Maxine succumbed.

"Well, I feel guilty that I didn't buy anything else," she whispered. "At least the ostriches will be happy to see us."

Indeed they were, a dozen of them forsaking the shade of their shelter and crowding the fence for treats when they saw the plastic bags. Mrs. Entwhistle and Maxine had to stand back to avoid their thrusting heads.

"Just toss the feed over the fence," Mrs. Entwhistle advised. "I think ostriches bite."

"Maaaaamaaa!" screamed a little boy at knee level. "She said they're os'riches, and they bite! But they're llamas, and llamas don't bite, do they? Mama Llama wouldn't bite, would she?"

His mother shot him a despairing look. "Well, honey, they really are ostriches, but you can pretend..." she began.

"Noooo! They're llamas!"

"Which one is Mama Llama?" Maxine asked, expertly short-circuiting a tantrum in the making. She bent down to look the child in the eyes.

"She ain't *here,*" he said, sticking out his lower lip. "She's in my book. She's Llama Llama's mama, and she don't bite!"

"No, of course not," Maxine murmured.

"You're mean!" the boy continued, jabbing a stubby finger in Mrs. Entwhistle's direction. "You're a big meanie!"

"Now, honey, don't be rude to the old lady," his mother said, pinching the bridge of her nose and rubbing her eyes. "Sorry, ma'am. He's overtired."

Mrs. Entwhistle was far from being offended; she was intrigued. She knelt to the little boy's level. "You say these llamas are in a book? Well, aren't you lucky to know these things! I bet your mother reads to you. I get mixed up about ostriches and llamas, so it's a good thing you're here to set me straight. Tell me about llamas. Are you sure they don't bite?"

"No, ma'am. They kick, though," the child said, restored to civility by her capitulation. "And they can run really, really, really fast."

"Good to know. Thank you for telling me about them.

You keep on reading books, you hear?" Mrs. Entwhistle struggled to her feet, grateful for a boost from Maxine. She smiled and waggled her fingers. "Enjoy the llamas. Bye-bye now."

She and Maxine were both laughing as they drove away. "Another example of how I've lost my touch with young'uns," Mrs. Entwhistle said. "I just seem to annoy 'em these days. Remind me to buy that Mama Llama book when we get home."

"Who will you read it to?" Maxine asked.

"Myself."

~*~

"Well, I'm standin' on the corner of Winslow, Arizona, and it's such a fine sight to see. It's a girl, my lord, in a flatbed Ford, slowin' down to take a look at me."

Mrs. Entwhistle and Maxine harmonized on the chorus of the Eagle's song. They sang it at full volume, because they were coming into Winslow itself.

"I never thought I'd actually see this little corner of the world," Maxine said with satisfaction.

"And lookee there." Mrs. Entwhistle pointed at a statue of a cowboy complete with guitar standing on the fabled corner ready for a photo op. "We have to take pictures," she said, pulling the car into a curbside parking spot.

First Maxine posed with the statue, then Mrs. Entwhistle, each of them taking several shots with their cell phone cameras. Maxine hailed a passerby and asked if he'd take pictures of the two of them. He complied gruffly.

"I guess the town's population gets tired of the whole thing," Maxine whispered to Mrs. Entwhistle as they arranged themselves on either side of the statue.

"They must not hate it too much; they have a Standin' on the Corner Festival every September according to that poster. Too bad we won't be here."

Mrs. Entwhistle reached up and draped her arm around the statue's shoulders just as the picture was taken. She was delighted with it when she viewed it in her camera. "Perfect!" she said. "I'm going to send it to Dex."

His response came promptly. "Huh? Where are you, and who's that supposed to be? Sam Houston? Davy Crockett?"

The ladies shook their heads in despair. "I guess he's too young," Maxine said.

"There's such a thing as being too young and too *ignorant*!" Mrs. Entwhistle sent the photo to Diane, and Tommy, but they didn't know the reference, either. She fired off a group text to all of them: "For heaven's sake! LOOK IT UP!"

They poked around the shops lining Winslow's main drag, but they were like every gift shop in every tourist town, and they soon grew bored.

"I guess we should be thinking about where we're going to spend the night," Mrs. Entwhistle said.

"The guidebook gives a great rating to La Posada Hotel." Maxine thumbed through her book and read aloud. "It was established by Fred Harvey, the man who brought white tablecloth dining to railroad cars back in the day. The architect was a woman by the name of Mary Elizabeth Jane Colter. La Posada means The Resting Place, and it's designed to resemble a rich hacienda. It has a wonderful restaurant, the Turquoise Room." She looked up. "What would you think about splurging, and spending the night there?"

Mrs. Entwhistle was tempted. "It's probably too expensive, but let's go take a look at it, anyway."

La Posada turned out to be the incarnation of their dreams of the Southwest. The spacious adobe building sat in splendor amid twelve acres of beautifully landscaped gardens. Even in the desert, the air was perfumed by flowers and cooled by the splash of fountains.

"Oh!" Maxine breathed.

"Ah!" Mrs. Entwhistle sighed. "I miss my yard. Not that my yard looks anything like *this*."

"Let's stay. I don't care what it costs, do you?"

"Every trip should have at least one splurge," Mrs. Entwhistle said.

Their room contained elaborate handmade wooden headboards and painted antique furniture. Maxine immediately stretched out on one of the beds.

"Perfect!" she declared.

They made reservations for an early dinner in the Turquoise Room and walked in the gardens until they found a shady spot to sit. They didn't welcome the interruption of Maxine's cell phone ringing, but it rang anyway. Maxine answered because she couldn't ignore a phone call. No matter how sternly Mrs. Entwhistle lectured her about not answering if she didn't recognize the caller, Maxine always answered. Mrs. Entwhistle got up and walked around to give her privacy. When she returned,

Maxine's face was streaked with tears.

"Why, Max, what's the matter?"

"It's my niece. That was her husband, Trey, on the phone. Lucy had the baby, a little boy, and there were complications. She has an infection, and both she and the baby have to remain in the hospital for now. Then they're all going to stay with Trey's mother in San Francisco for a couple of weeks. It's their first baby, after all, and Trey sounded scared, like he needed his Mom. He said if we hadn't started yet, not to come because they won't be home."

"Oh, I'm so sorry. Is the baby okay?"

"He said yes, just a bit small. The main concern is Lucy; she's not able to care for the baby alone just yet. I don't blame them for doing what they need to do, but gosh, I'm disappointed. That was the whole point of this trip, to help with the baby, and now I won't even get to see him. San Francisco is 'way up at the other end of California."

"We could drive on up there," Mrs. Entwhistle said hesitantly. It really was a long way, and the trip had been exhaustingly eventful so far. She wasn't sure she was up for much more.

"No, I got the impression the family wants to be left alone right now." Maxine dried her tears and squared her shoulders. "Never mind. What can't be cured must be endured."

They sat silently for a few minutes, then both spoke at once.

"What would you think--?"

"Maxine, what if we--?"

"You go ahead," Maxine said.

"What if we went home now? Would you be upset if we turned around before we reach California? We're not far--it's only about another 500 miles or so--but there's not much point in sticking to our original plan now."

Maxine's face brightened. "You know, I was about to say the very same thing. I'm tired, and I know you are, too. It's been quite a trip, and I'll admit it--I'm a little homesick."

"Me, too. I miss Roger and wonder how Dex is doing. It's time to turn on the furnace, and I'm worried that I didn't get it serviced before we left. Then there's the autumn yard work. Dex said Booger mulched the flower beds, but I doubt he cleaned out the annuals for winter."

"I'd like to get up in the morning and have a cup of tea at my own kitchen table."

They smiled at each other. “It doesn’t take much to satisfy us, does it?” Mrs. Entwhistle said.

“It’s one of our best traits,” Maxine said.

Sex in a Pan

"We've only been gone a few days; do you think we'd dare stop and see Delilah and J.J. on our way home, or is it too soon?" Mrs. Entwhistle asked.

"I guess they'd be surprised if we turned up again," Maxine said hesitantly, "but I'd love to see that baby one more time."

"Let's call."

Delilah answered on the first ring.

"It's Mrs. Entwhistle, Delilah. Our plans have changed, and we're heading home instead of going on to California. We wondered if it would be convenient for us to stop for a short visit on our way."

"Why, I'd love it, and I know Jean would, too," Delilah said. "She's right here. What's that, Aunt Jean? She says she owes you a favor, anyway."

"Me? I don't recall doing a favor," Mrs. Entwhistle said.

"Yes, you did." Jean's voice filled the car. For such a small person, she had a surprisingly loud voice. Mrs. Entwhistle could relate, since her own voice frequently rose to an unacceptable volume. "You girls come on and plan to spend the night again."

"Thanks, but we wouldn't dream of putting you out...."

"Nonsense! I haven't even changed the sheets from your first visit yet. Take your time; we'll expect you when we see you."

The connection was broken. Mrs. Entwhistle shrugged; Maxine smiled. They were in for another night in the tower room. "I hope that ghost doesn't know we're coming."

They settled down for the three-hour drive back to Glenrio. This time the old town seemed more mellow than sad, like an old friend a bit down on his luck. They drove past the deserted buildings with a feeling of homecoming and pulled into Jean's driveway. The improbable house looked back at them with blank eyes; then the door flew open and Jean and Delilah barreled out to greet them.

"Hi, Maxine, Mrs. Entwhistle," Delilah called, waving energetically.

"Come on in here, you two!" Jean bellowed.

They found themselves hugged, gripped and propelled up the steps, across the front porch, and into the wide central hallway. A mouth-watering smell of something baking greeted them.

"You're just in time for tea," Jean said. "It's all laid out in the dining room."

Once again, Mrs. Entwhistle marveled at the beautifully set table and helped herself to an immodest portion of scones and whipped cream.

"Where's that baby?" she asked Delilah with her mouth full.

"He's taking a nap in his crib," she said proudly. J.J.'s days of sleeping in motel dresser drawers were over. "He's adjusting beautifully to being here, and I swear he's grown just in the last couple of days."

"And you, Jean? How is it having your niece and a new baby in the house?" Maxine asked.

"Love it," Jean answered succinctly. "This big, old, house has been too quiet since my husband died. I had nothing to think about but redecorating. Drove my handyman nuts with the painting. Now I have a baby to rock and a daughter--well, she feels like my daughter--to look after. Tell them about school, Delilah."

"Jean's already found me a tutor," Delilah said. "He'll come to the house and help me catch up on what I missed so I can keep up with my grade at school. Maybe for my senior year, I can commute back and forth to the high school in Ray. It's twenty-three miles, but that's not considered a long drive around here. Aunt Jean's going to teach me to drive her Cadillac, and she said she'll baby-sit J.J. while I'm in class."

Mrs. Entwhistle sighed with relief. She'd been worried about Delilah missing so much class work. It sounded like Jean shared that worry and would make sure the girl graduated from high school.

"Delilah will get an education," Jean said, nodding her head decisively. "She can take care of her child and go to school, including college. Plenty of others have done it before her. Fortunately, I've got money and nothing better to do with it. Money greases the wheels of whatever you want to do."

"Oh, Aunt Jean, you're the best!" Delilah reached over and gave her aunt a one-armed hug.

"What about your parents?" Mrs. Entwhistle asked. "Have you talked to them?

"Daddy called last night. Mother still hasn't relented. But you know what? I don't want to go back even if she says I can. I love staying here with Jean."

J.J. announced his return to consciousness at that moment and, in the way of babies the world over, took up all their attention for the rest of the evening. Mrs. Entwhistle and Maxine declared he'd grown and was even more adorable than before. Delilah beamed proudly, and Jean hovered over the two of them like the grandmother she felt herself to be.

"I never thought I'd have this experience," she confided to Mrs. Entwhistle. "Had no kids of my own, you know. Just not built for it. But now, to have Delilah and J.J., it's like I have a daughter and grandson. Helen Martin is a stupid, selfish woman, and Jim is too scared of her to make her behave. They're missing out on their only grandchild. Well, their loss is my gain."

It wasn't until bedtime that Mrs. Entwhistle remembered what Delilah had said about Jean owing them thanks for a favor.

"What did we do?" she asked her hostess.

"Why, you let me know there was a window broken in the storage room in the tower," Jean said. "There was the coldest draft coming from under the door at night, but I seldom go up there, and I just hadn't noticed. There was even an owl's nest in the corner of the room. Good thing you gals didn't hear any hooting when you stayed up there--it would have scared you to death. Well, it's all fixed now."

Mrs. Entwhistle saw Maxine turning away to hide a smile, and she smiled herself.

"So much for my psychic powers," she said as they made their way up the stairs to their aerie. "Thank goodness I didn't mention it in an article for the newspaper. Least said, soonest mended."

The next morning was a rerun of the first--no hostess and no breakfast. Delilah managed tea and toast for them while tending to J.J., and then the ladies said goodbye again.

"I swanee," Mrs. Entwhistle said, wiping her eyes as they drove away. "That young'un seems like one of my own after what-all we've been through together. J.J. is the only baby I ever delivered. I wonder if he'll ever get to know that. I wonder if I'll ever see him again."

"We'll keep in touch," Maxine promised, a little misty herself. "Maybe she'll come visit and bring the baby to see us one day. Wouldn't that be something?"

Route 66 hummed and spun under their wheels. The landscape was sandy and monotonous, and the thrum of the big car's engine was a lullaby.

"Is there anything to see in this stretch?" Mrs. Entwhistle asked, rubbing her sleepy eyes. "I could do with a stop." Her stomach grumbled menacingly. "And food," she added.

Maxine had accumulated a number of tourist brochures, and she paged through them. "No, I don't think we're near any scenic sites. Let's stop, though, and get a piece of pie at the next place we see. I think pie is what we need."

But it was many miles before they saw a small roadside diner, its neon sign rendered almost invisible by the bright sunshine. "Chez Randy," it said dimly. Mrs. Entwhistle pulled in, her mouth watering at the thought of pie. What was it about traveling that made a person so hungry all the time--and for the most fattening kind of food! At this rate, she'd have to go through her front door sideways.

They were the only customers, although the clock on

the wall said it was lunch time. That clock was in the shape of a cat, and its tail swung back and forth to mark each second. Mrs. Entwhistle had a flashback of watching an identical clock in her childhood dentist's office. It was supposed to distract her while her teeth were tortured with that old-time fire and brimstone drill. She could smell the hot smoke.

The diner was one room with a long Formica counter and peeling vinyl swivel stools bolted to the floor. The day's specials were noted on hand-printed cards tacked over the kitchen pass-through. An ancient man shuffled out, wiping his hands on an apron so filthy Mrs. Entwhistle had to look away. She picked up a menu and joined Maxine in perusing it.

"What'll you have?" the old man asked indifferently, not making eye contact.

"I'll have the cherry pie," Maxine said. "A' la mode."

The old man heaved a sigh. "Out," he said.

"Okay. Well, then the apple pie?"

"Out."

"Chocolate?"

"Nope."

A voice from the kitchen: "Dad! Stop messing with the ladies. I'll be right there."

The owner of the voice turned out to be one of the handsomest men either Mrs. Entwhistle or Maxine had ever seen. They exchanged round-eyed glances when he appeared, his spotless chef's whites matched by his gleaming smile.

"Oh, my," Maxine breathed. "Uh, what *do* you have, then? I mean, to eat. I mean, pie."

"We're all out of pie today," the young man said with a heart-breaking smile. "But may I bring you something special? Will you allow me to surprise you?"

"I'm sure it'll be just what we need," Mrs. Entwhistle said. "To eat! What we need to eat!" She was equally as star-struck as Maxine. "I'm Cora Entwhistle," she said, extending her hand over the counter. "And this is my friend, Maxine."

"It's a pleasure to meet you, ladies. I'm Chef Randy, and we're delighted to have you in our bistro today."

The old man snorted and rolled his eyes. "It ain't a bistro, it's a damn diner. I done tol' you that about a thousand times. And you're just plain Randy, always have been, always will be."

"You're right, Dad, you're right, but someday it'll be a real bistro, and people will drive for miles to eat my cooking."

"Illusions of grander," the old man said. "Ever since you went to cookin' school, you've had them illusions of grander."

"You mean *delusions of grandeur*, Dad, and I guess I do," Chef Randy said, patting his parent gently on the back. "Now why don't you sit down with these two nice ladies, and I'll bring you a treat, too."

"Is it what I think it is?" The old man's cloudy eyes brightened.

"It is, Dad, but don't tell. Let's surprise them."

The dessert Chef Randy put before them a few minutes later was a layered confection that made Mrs. Entwhistle's mouth water before she even tasted it. When she did, it did not disappoint.

"Cream cheese... mmmmm!" Maxine said. "And whipped cream!"

"And pudding... ahh!... and pecans...." Words failed Mrs. Entwhistle, but her mouth was too full to talk, anyway.

Randy's father had removed his apron and seated himself beside them at the counter. He, too, was head-down over his plate. “The boy knows how to make some good stuff,” he mumbled, around a huge bite. “I ain’t got all my teeth, but I can eat this. I have a little trouble with them pecans, but it’s worth it.”

Chef Randy stood on the other side of the counter beaming. He poured cups of dark, fragrant coffee and set them in front of their plates. “Here, cut the sweetness with this.”

“It’s delicious,” Maxine said. “Would you consider sharing the recipe? What’s it called?”

“Sex in a Pan,” Randy said.

“I beg your pardon?”

“That’s what it’s called--Sex in a Pan. You like it?”

“I don’t think I’ve ever liked anything better. Including sex outside the pan,” Maxine confessed shyly.

Laughing, Randy disappeared into the kitchen. When he returned, he handed over a neatly-written recipe card. “I’m happy to share the recipe,” he said. “It’s not a fancy cordon bleu dish, but people around here aren’t going to order Bananas Foster. I’m embarrassed, I’ll admit it, to use instant pudding mix, but folks love it. It was my Mom’s recipe, and she’d serve it every Friday night. We were always packed on Friday nights."

Maxine and Mrs. Entwhistle put their heads together and read:

Sex in a Pan

1 cup chopped pecans

2 tablespoons granulated sugar

1 cup flour

½ cup butter, melted

1 8oz. package cream cheese

½ cup powdered sugar

1 cup whipped cream

1 5.1 oz. instant vanilla pudding mixed with 1 cup of milk

1 5.1 oz. instant chocolate pudding mixed with 1 cup of milk

2 cups whipped cream

Preheat oven to 350 degrees. Mix pecans, granulated sugar, butter, and flour. Press into baking dish and bake for 25 minutes.

Mix pudding mixes in separate bowls with 1 cup of milk each. Chill in refrigerator.

Beat cream cheese, powdered sugar, and 1 cup whipped cream until light and fluffy.

After the crust cools, spread cream cheese mixture evenly over it, followed by a layer of chocolate pudding, then vanilla pudding, then whipped cream. Top with shaved chocolate if desired.

Refrigerate overnight.

"It's not all that difficult," Mrs. Entwhistle said. "I'm going to make it for Dex when we get home."

"I'm going to make it for me," Maxine said, running her finger around the plate to scoop up the last lick of whipped cream.

The Art of Intuition

"Do you think I should include the Sex in a Pan recipe in my column for the *Pantograph*?" Mrs. Entwhistle asked.

"Not just yet, let's make it a couple of times for pot lucks before we share the recipe."

Mrs. Entwhistle and Maxine were in their nightgowns, wet hair wrapped in towel turbans as they settled in for the night at the Best Western near Elk City, Oklahoma. They'd stayed there during their trip out, so it felt familiar. The drive home was more leisurely, inspired less by the spirit of exploration and more by a bitter-sweet satisfaction in being homeward-bound.

Mrs. Entwhistle was staring at her laptop, willing

words to appear on the screen. So far, nothing. "I'd like to tell folks about Chez Randy, just in case anybody from home gets out this way. Randy needs the business if he's ever going to fulfill his dream of having a real restaurant."

"Just write about how good the food was, and how nice Randy was. Even his dad loosened up after he had Sex in a Pan."

"Well, who wouldn't? He didn't need all his teeth for it. That was a major selling point."

"Say, Cora, what about Marty?"

"The little kitten we left at the vet's on the way out? What about her?"

"Tomorrow when Dr. Carroway's office opens, we need to go see about her."

"I wonder if she survived. She was in pretty bad shape when we left her, and that was only a couple of weeks ago. She hasn't had much time to recover, *if* she's going to recover. What do you want to do if she's still alive?"

Maxine sighed. "I don't quite know. I'd love to adopt her, but it might be a struggle to have a sick, fragile cat in the car as we travel."

Mrs. Entwhistle privately thought it sounded like

hell on wheels--literally--but if that was what Maxine wanted, then so be it. “If you want her, Max, and if the vet thinks she’s well enough to travel, then of course we can manage. What’s a tiny scrap of a cat after the trip we’ve had?”

“I guess we’d better see her before we decide anything.”

The next morning they were in Dr. Carroway’s office when it opened at nine, explaining to the receptionist that no, they didn’t have an appointment, they were just passing through and wanted to check on a kitten they’d left in Dr. Carroway’s care.

“You must mean Marty,” the girl said. “We kinda thought you’d never come back for him.”

“Him? We thought it was a female.”

“Nope, Marty is a tomcat. Oh, I just heard Dr. Carroway come in. Let me tell him you’re here.”

A few minutes later, they were ushered into a treatment room where Dr. Carroway stood holding a plump, tiger-striped, orange kitten against his white coat.

“Ladies,” he said, depositing the kitten on the examining table with a flourish. “Ta-da! May I present Martin the Magnificent!"

"My land!" Mrs. Entwhistle breathed. "Will you look at that?"

The pitiful scrap of fur had been transformed. Martin was now a healthy six-week old kitten with clear eyes, shining fur, and a perky little tail. He looked them over and said, "Mew." Mrs. Entwhistle thought it sounded a lot like "Meh." Marty was unimpressed by his benefactors. He was a cat, after all.

"How did you manage such a change in such a short time?" Maxine asked.

"I had a mother cat with a new litter. She adopted Marty as one of her own and fed him with her babies. It was exactly what he needed. He's a survivor, our Marty, and he just needed a little motherly TLC to thrive."

"Do you think he's healthy enough to travel?" Maxine asked.

"Depends. How far are you going?"

"We're headed home. Just another couple days, and we'll be there."

"Then I think Martin could withstand the trip. He's ready to be weaned and has already been eating a little kibble. If you have a cat carrier, a litter box, and food bowls, I think he'll be okay."

"We still have the box and litter we bought for him before, and we'll get a carrier. You've done a wonderful job of pulling him through. I really didn't expect him to live," Maxine said. "How much do I owe you?"

"You paid in advance, remember? You don't owe me a thing. I'm happy I could help. But listen, if you don't want him, I'd be happy to keep him. He's a good little cat."

"I appreciate everything you've done for him, and I do want him. He'll always remind me of an unforgettable trip."

Marty settled into travel mode with no problems and proved to be an amusing companion. He slept in a boneless puddle of fur part of the time, and when he was awake he climbed around in the car. Occasionally he landed in a lap or on a shoulder where he allowed himself to be stroked and made much of for a few minutes. His raspy purr filled the car with contentment. Maxine fell more and more in love with her little souvenir.

"Do you think Marty is a proper name for this cat?" she asked. "It's okay while he's a kitten, but maybe it isn't dignified enough for a grown cat."

"He's going to get big. I predict he'll be a majestic tomcat with a string of lady friends, and then you can call him Martin. Meanwhile, just stick with Marty. It's a versatile name."

Mrs. Entwhistle had been having guilty thoughts on another subject. "I haven't picked up one thing for my kids on this trip," she said to Maxine. "I'm sure they'll be expecting gifts, and you know how I hate to shop. I just haven't gotten around to it, and now we're on our way home, and I'm empty-handed. You've at least got a cat."

"True, but I'm not sharing him with anyone. What do you think your family would like?"

"Something authentic and native-made, not cheesy gift shop souvenirs from China. I wish I could find a place that sold Native American crafts."

"That shouldn't be too hard. We're approaching Tulsa, and there are bound to be gift shops there. Let's keep our eyes peeled."

But the big city's outskirts seemed to contain mostly pawn shops and Laundromats. Maxine checked her phone for information. She found the Cherokee National Welcome Center was located in Tulsa, and it had a gift shop.

"Here's a good one," she said.

The address was punched into their GPS, and Mrs. Entwhistle navigated her way to it. Once inside they were impressed by the beauty of the items on display. They wandered the aisles, marveling at the baskets, sculptures, and jewelry. Mrs. Entwhistle wasn't one to linger too long over shopping, however, and she quickly selected several gifts for her children, and grandchildren.

"This stuff is pricey, but it's the real deal," she said, lining up her purchases on the counter. She'd chosen a woven honeysuckle basket, a turquoise money clip, beaded earrings, tee shirts in various sizes, and for the youngest, a little carved wooden buffalo. But she wasn't quite finished.

"Excuse me just a minute; I want to get one more thing."

When she returned, she carried a black velvet box in which nestled a silver and turquoise ring, daintily and beautifully made. It cost more than everything else she'd chosen put together, and it didn't look at all like something she'd wear.

"Why, Cora, I've never known you to wear a ring except for your wedding band," Maxine said.

"Oh, it's not for me," Mrs. Entwhistle replied. She

refused to say another word, only shaking her head with a smile at Max's questions.

The Accident

Screeching tires and a loud percussion preceded Mrs. Entwhistle's intimate acquaintance with the airbag. It exploded in her face, knocking off her glasses. For a moment, she couldn't take in what had just happened.

We were riding along; I was dozing; Maxine was driving. Maxine!

"Max, are you okay?"

Silence. Mrs. Entwhistle pushed the airbag out of the way and looked over at the driver's side of the car. The seat was empty, and the door hung open. Fumbling in panic, she unclicked her seat belt and tried to open her door, but it wouldn't budge. The car was almost on its side at an odd, disorienting angle.

"Max!" she called again and again got silence.

Somehow she managed to scramble over the console in the center of the seats and slide across to the open driver's side door. But when she looked out, she was looking into space. The car hung off the side of a steep embankment and her movements caused it to creak and shift as pebbles pattered to the ground. Mrs. Entwhistle froze. There was no way out except a twenty-foot drop, and the car was unstable. Below she saw Maxine's inert body huddled on the ground. If the car fell, it would land directly on her.

Mrs. Entwhistle's ears still rang from the airbag's punch, and she squinted without her glasses. Fighting back fear, she sat still and thought hard. They were on Route 66. Surely a passing car would spot them and stop to help. There had been very little traffic so far, but it was only six in the morning. She and Maxine had awakened early and eagerly started the final leg of their homeward journey.

Inching her fingers carefully behind her, she felt for her phone in the cup holder where she'd wedged it, surrounded by maps and packages of chewing gum. Yes! It hadn't gone skittering to the floor in the crash. She eased the phone around in front of her and punched 911. Nothing. No little bars at the top of the screen; no cell service in the area.

A small *mew* sounded from the back seat. Cautiously turning her head, she was face to face with Marty peering at her from his cat carrier. "What the heck?" he seemed to be thinking. Mrs. Entwhistle was thankful he was in the carrier and hadn't been thrown around the car. Meanwhile, how could she help Maxine?

"Cora?" The voice was a weak croak, but it was unmistakably Maxine's.

"Oh, thank goodness!" Mrs. Entwhistle exclaimed. "Can you move, Max?"

"I--I think so."

"Then get out from under the car. Take your time, don't hurt yourself, but get clear in case the car falls. Can you do that?"

"Yes. I'll have to crawl. I don't think I can put weight on my right ankle."

"Well, crawl then. Just get out of the way."

Mrs. Entwhistle watched her friend inch through the brush on her hands and knees.

"Do you think there are snakes down here?" Max

called.

"No, absolutely not. Wrong time of year," Mrs. Entwhistle lied. She felt certain Maxine needed that lie at the moment.

"Okay, I think I'm clear now. What should I do next?"

"I don't dare move," Mrs. Entwhistle said. "If I stir even a little, the car shifts. I tried my cell phone, but there's no service here. I'm afraid it's up to you to get up to the road and flag down help."

Maxine looked at the steep embankment and grimaced. There was no way she could climb it, but maybe she could crawl up hand over hand by hanging onto the scrubby vegetation. Her first attempt resulted in a double handful of weeds and an ignominious slide back to the ground. She tried again and made it about halfway before losing her grip and rolling back to the bottom where she lay panting.

Mrs. Entwhistle watched, her heart pounding, feeling completely helpless. She wasn't hurt and could have made it up that escarpment without much trouble, but she didn't dare even move. Poor Max was left to rescue the both of them, hampered by an ankle that Mrs. Entwhistle could see, even from a distance, was swelling rapidly.

"Max? Are you okay?"

"Yes, just resting a minute."

"Remember that movie we laughed at so much, that Jack Lemmon movie where he, and Alan Arkin are running to dodge bullets and he keeps saying, 'Serpentine! Serpentine!"

"Yes, I remember, it was *The Inlaws*." Maxine had learned long ago not to question where her friend's mind went.

"Try that; try going up at an angle. You'll have to cover more ground, but it won't seem as steep."

Maxine tried again, making her way at a forty-five degree angle, clawing at the undergrowth as she went.

"Now go the other way," Mrs. Entwhistle called.

There were a couple of breath-stopping moments when Maxine slipped and had to scramble to hang on, but finally she made it to the top. Mrs. Entwhistle saw her swollen ankle disappear over the edge.

"I'm here." Max's voice floated down just as the car gave a convulsive shudder and slid a few feet. An outcropping of rock saved it from plunging all the way to the bottom. Mrs. Entwhistle froze, feeling sweat trickling down her sides.

"Okay, I hear you. I daren't move, though. The car just slid a little bit."

Mrs. Entwhistle felt the vibration before she heard the sound of a mighty engine roaring towards them. She clutched the steering wheel with white-knuckled hands, fearing the car would be dislodged and make its final fall. She heard Maxine yelling and could imagine her standing at the edge of the road waving her arms. The engine slowed. Mrs. Entwhistle heard excited chatter, but couldn't make out the words. A deep voice shouted down to her.

"Are you okay? I've got a CB radio, and I'll call for help."

"Yes, I'm fine, but I don't dare make a move or this car will fall. Who are you? Is Maxine all right?"

"I'm Sam. Your friend flagged my truck down. She's okay except for her ankle and a few scrapes and bruises. She's sitting in the truck right now, so she's safe. You just sit tight; help's on the way."

As if I could do anything but sit tight. And how in the world are they going to get me out of here without the car falling?

It seemed forever until the fire rescue unit arrived. She heard the siren as they approached, heard it gradually dying as they arrived. Again the vibrations of the truck on the road sent a shiver of fear through her, but the car remained on its perch. If she carefully leaned forward a few inches, she could see legs and feet lined up above her at the top of the embankment. She didn't know if she was visible, but she risked sticking her arm out the door and gave a tiny wave with just her fingers.

"We'll get you out, ma'am," one of them called. "Just sit tight."

Again with the sitting tight. Do they think I'm going to dance the hornpipe?

The biggest problem, the head of the rescue squad shouted down to her, was that most of the car was already over the edge. "We don't have much to get ahold of," he said. "We're going to try to get a cable around the back axle. Where are you in the car?

"Driver's seat," Mrs. Entwhistle said.

"Do you have the seat belt on?"

"No."

"Please put it on now, if you can. It'll help if the car… Just put it on, okay?"

"Okay."

She heard clanking and felt the car shudder beneath

her. A seat belt didn't seem like much insurance against a twenty-foot drop. She hoped Maxine had stayed in the truck and wasn't watching. It would be a sight Max would never be unable to unsee if the car fell. Marty's angry meows sounded from the cat carrier. He was complaining about the lack of room service, no doubt. *Little do you know, my boy, how much you have to complain about!* Mrs. Entwhistle felt a lurch and heard a cheer.

"We've got the car hooked," her rescuer shouted "but it's still pretty mobile. We don't think it's secure enough to safely climb to you, so we're going to lift you out in a harness. Now here's what I want you to do. Get over to the passenger's side of the car, and put the window down."

"The automatic windows aren't working," Mrs. Entwhistle said. "Not with the car turned off, and I already tried that door – it won't open."

"Okay. I can see that the driver's side door is open. Is that where you're sitting?"

"Yes."

"We're going to drop a harness over to that side. Put it on."

The harness appeared, dangling in front of her. It looked like an impossibly complicated web of straps.

How in the world was she to get into it? But a fit young firefighter was scrambling down the embankment. He stood below her and talked her through it, although she kept warning him not to stand below the car. She thought the only thing worse than being crushed herself would be the last-minute knowledge that she was taking someone to glory with her.

"Don't worry, ma'am, I can get out of the way in a hurry. You just concentrate on putting that harness on."

It was tricky, getting out of the seat belt and squirming into the harness. Her every movement made the car shiver and shift, causing her to pause for heart-stopping moments. Finally she buckled the last strap, not at all sure she'd gotten it right. There were more important things to think about, but she spared a moment to wish with all her heart that she'd worn trousers that day.

"What's your name?" Mrs. Entwhistle asked the young man below her. "My name is Cora Entwhistle. I think we should know each other's names."

"I'm Dave, ma'am, pleased to meet you. We've done plenty of rescues, and we know what we're doing. You can trust us to get you out of there, but you're going to have to be very brave and help us. Now I want you to scoot over to the edge of the seat and jump out of the car."

"Jump? Dave, I'm seventy-nine years of age. I don't jump."

"You do today, ma'am. When you jump clear of the car, the harness will catch you and the crew will pull you up."

"What about Marty?"

"Marty? Is there another person in the car?"

"No, Marty's a cat. I can't just leave him. He's in a carrier."

There was a conference among her rescuers as they took in this new information. The consensus was that Marty should wait for rescue until Mrs. Entwhistle was safe.

"No, I'm not going without him," Mrs. Entwhistle said firmly. "This is Maxine's kitten, and he's been through a lot. I won't leave him behind."

No amount of shouted entreaties could sway her. She felt if they could rescue her, they could surely rescue a little scrap of a kitten, too.

"I'll carry the cat when I jump," she said decisively.

Her rescuers weren't happy, but they finally had to accept it. With strength she didn't know she had, Mrs. Entwhistle reached back, grabbed Marty's carrier, and hauled it over the seat. She hugged it to her chest with both arms, shut her eyes, and launched herself into mid-air.

She twisted round and round, completely disoriented by the whirling. Eyes tightly closed she clung to Marty, who was making his feelings about the trip into space known. A paw reached through the carrier and razor-sharp kitten claws raked her arm. Then a sharp jerk propelled her even higher. She expected to hear the car fall, but the cable around the axle held. There was a grinding, tearing sound as more rocks were dislodged. Her shoes fell off, and her skirt blew up over her head. It was just as well she didn't hear the whirring of the news camera as it followed her ascent.

I See London, I See France

Maxine really needed to go to the hospital to have her ankle seen to, but Mrs. Entwhistle felt she had no such need herself. Everything seemed to be in working order, except for a couple of sore ribs from the harness and a row of bloody scratches on her arm from the cat. Both she and Marty had come through their adventure relatively unscathed, although Marty was yowling and could wait no longer to get to his litter box. An unmistakable aroma rose from his carrier.

The paramedics insisted Mrs. Entwhistle at least climb into the ambulance for a check of her vital signs. They were fine, as she'd known they would be once she got out of that car. Maxine was a different story. Her face had an alarming lack of color, and her eyes kept filling with tears.

"I'm so sorry, Cora, that I caused our wonderful trip end this way," she said.

"Max, don't you apologize! I know you didn't mean to have an accident. That's why they're called accidents. What caused you to run off the road, anyway?"

"I just remember seeing something run in front of me. It seemed as big as Roger, but the guys here say it was probably a jackrabbit. I instinctively swerved to miss it, and the next thing I knew, I woke up on the ground."

"Didn't you have your seat belt on?"

Maxine's pale face pinked up with a blush. "Well, no, I'd just undone it because it was cutting me across the throat. There was nobody else on the road, but I shouldn't have taken it off even for a moment."

Mrs. Entwhistle knew that because of Maxine's short stature, the seatbelt hit her in an uncomfortable place. Max'd tried pads and adjustors of all sorts, but seatbelts did tend to go right across her throat even when she was seated on her driving cushion

"The important thing is that you're alive," Mrs.

Entwhistle said, suddenly weak with fright. The thought of losing her friend made her feel overwhelmed and tearful. How would she ever get along without Maxine's enduring friendship and support? She shook her head to dislodge the tears and fought her weakness in typical fashion, by taking action.

"Well, for heaven's sake!" she said to the nearest paramedic. "Let's get this show on the road. We have to get our luggage out of that car, and figure out how we're going to get home."

This time the siren screamed directly overhead as the ambulance rolled toward the nearest hospital. Mrs. Entwhistle sat back quietly, allowing the medics room to monitor their patient. It was up to her to think what to do next. She knew she could call Diane or Tommy and they'd come right away, but just at the moment she didn't feel up to making that call. Her head ached, and another onslaught of smells drifted from Marty's carrier which she still held in her lap. Her stomach gave a lurch.

"I don't think you'll be allowed to take that cat into the hospital waiting room," one of the medics said. "That's one stinky cat."

"Well, he can't help it; he's just a baby," Mrs. Entwhistle said. She reached her hand in to pet the little cat who was mewing pitifully. "He's hungry, and he's made a mess in his carrier because nobody has taken him out and put him in his litter box."

The female paramedic, whose nametag said "G. Smithers," looked sympathetic. She was a bleached-out, lonesome-looking woman with a lazy eye that wandered off to the left.

"I love cats," Smithers said. "Had one until recently; I had to put her down last week. She was old and sick, but I sure miss her."

She paused and looked at Maxine speculatively. "Say, could I look after this kitten for you until you get squared away? I'm going off duty as soon as we deliver you two to the hospital; it's the end of my shift. I could take him home, feed him and get him cleaned up. When you're ready just call me. We cat ladies have to stick together."

"Oh, would you really do that? It would be so kind!" Maxine said. "I've been worrying about what we'd do with him. Marty has had a tough start. First his mother was killed when he was too young to be weaned, then he had to stay at the vet's for a couple of weeks and now this. He's going to use up his nine lives before he even grows up. I would be so grateful if you'd look after him for a bit. It shouldn't take us long to figure out what to do next."

Maxine learned that the G. on Smithers' nametag stood for Gloria, and she and Gloria talked cats for the rest of the trip. They exchanged phone numbers as the ambulance pulled into the emergency room bay, and Gloria gave Maxine a careful hug before she departed with Marty's carrier in hand.

Two nurses waited to escort Maxine's stretcher inside. Mrs. Entwhistle climbed down unaided and went to sit in the waiting room. She gratefully accepted a cup of coffee from a Pink Lady volunteer and settled down in front of a television to watch the noon news. It felt like she'd been out of touch with events for years. No telling what had happened.

She heard all about a local election that had just taken place. Mrs. Entwhistle had no interest in the various candidates or their margins of victory or defeat. She settled back in her chair and sipped coffee, allowing her mind to start processing the events of the morning. Her attention was jerked back to the screen when she saw a woman flying through the air in a harness. The woman's skirt was up around her ears, her underpants were on full display, and her bare feet dangled like...like chicken feet. For a split second, Mrs. Entwhistle felt a pang of sisterly sympathy. Then, like a jab with a very sharp stick, the realization hit her.

"Oh, my God! That's me!" She said it aloud before she

could stop herself.

A few of the other waiting room inhabitants looked curiously from her to the screen. Fortunately, they were all preoccupied with their own problems and didn't have much interest in hers. By the time she blinked, her image was gone and the commentator had moved on to another story. She drew a deep breath of relief that her face hadn't been on view and sent out an earnest prayer that the story would remain local. The thought of folks back home seeing her in such disarray made her shudder. What, for instance, if Booger were to see that? She bet his crush on her would be gone in an instant. In spite of all that had just happened, Mrs. Entwhistle's sense of the ridiculous was tickled, and her mouth turned up at the corners. She couldn't wait to tell Maxine.

Woo-Woo

"Oh, poor ladies! Poor ladies!"

Mrs. Entwhistle was sitting beside the stretcher in Maxine's curtained cubicle in the Emergency Room. Rapid footsteps approached, the curtains were thrust aside, and there stood Mr. and Mrs. Patel.

"We saw the story about the accident on the news, and we knew right away it was you. Because you have such an unusual name," Mr. Patel said tactfully.

Mrs. Entwhistle shook her head to think what else the Patels had seen of her on the news.

Mrs. Patel was patting both Mrs. Entwhistle and Maxine, one with each hand. "Oh, poor ladies," she repeated softly with each pat. "You will come to us, of course. We are close by, only a few miles. Your room is ready. What is wrong with your ankle, Maxine? Is it broken?"

"No, just sprained, the doctor said." Maxine looked uncertainly at the large boot strapped to her foot. "He said I could walk on it with this boot. I just can't believe you've come to our rescue. I didn't even realize we were near your place."

"But you are," Mr. Patel said, "and we have our own in-house physician to care for you."

"Your own physician?" Mrs. Entwhistle repeated.

"Oh, yes. Our son, Sanjay, is home for a visit. You remember, we told you about him. He is a medical student at Yale University," Mrs. Patel said proudly.

"Of course we remember," Maxine said, "It's wonderful that he's home, but we wouldn't dream of taking precious time away from his visit."

"Please. You would be doing us a favor. We think he is bored, you see. There is nothing for him to do here, and he is used to a much faster pace. You will give him a purpose and a chance to show off his skills for us."

"But--"

"No, please, we won't hear of anything else. Shyam, go get the car. I'll see to the discharge papers," Mrs. Patel said. Her sari swished as she bustled off to the nurses' station.

"No point in arguing with Anjali," Mr. Patel said, smiling fondly at his wife's retreating back.

Mrs. Entwhistle and Maxine both shrugged. "Well, we've been kidnapped before," Maxine said. "We should be getting used to it."

The young man who met the car when they pulled into the Patel Paradise wore a weighty frown. His coal-black brows drew together over liquid brown eyes. "I am Dr. Patel," he announced.

The ladies gave him a tentative pass for his pomposity. He was the son of the lovely Anjali and Shyam; how bad could he be?

But it turned out he could be pretty bad. He rapped out orders to his parents in a manner that made Mrs. Entwhistle want to belt him. He immediately removed the boot from Maxine's foot and rewrapped her ankle, issuing instructions as he did so.

"Madam, you must keep your foot higher than your heart. Ice, Mother, STAT! Father, remove the pillows from another room. I need them for a prop."

His parents hurried to obey. Maxine started to protest. "Oh, really, it's just a sprain." But Dr. Patel would have none of it.

"A sprain can be more difficult to heal than a clean break," he pronounced. "I must insist that you comply with my treatment."

"Uh, what year of medical school are you in?" Mrs. Entwhistle asked.

"I will begin my internship when I return to Yale. I have been awarded a spot at Yale New Haven Hospital," he said proudly.

"Congratulations," Mrs. Entwhistle said. "But you haven't really treated patients yet, right?"

"Well, of course, not in a regular sense, no, not yet. But I assure you, my training is extensive."

"I'm sure it is, and I'm sure you're a wonderful physician." Mrs. Entwhistle carefully made her voice neutral to keep the laughter out. She didn't dare meet Maxine's eye.

"Here, Sanjay, here is the ice," Mrs. Patel said, hurrying into the room with an ice bag.

"And here are the pillows," Mr. Patel said.

Maxine's ankle was duly iced and propped. She was

brought a cup of steaming tea by Mrs. Patel and offered the daily newspaper by Mr. Patel. The young doctor-to-be made fussy little adjustments, but finally there was no more that could be done for her. The Patels backed out of the room fluttering their fingers goodbye, with promises of a wonderful dinner in the offing.

Mrs. Entwhistle and Maxine were glad of the chance to be alone for a few minutes. A lot had happened in one short day, and they needed to figure out what to do next.

"Do you think you'll be able to travel tomorrow?" Mrs. Entwhistle asked.

"Oh, of course. The question is how. Do you know where my car is?" Maxine asked.

"The last time I saw it, it was hanging off the side of the road with a cable hooked to the axle. I expect it's been towed somewhere. Will you be very upset if it's totaled? Even if it's repairable, it will take some time, and we can't stay with the Patels that long. I could call Tommy to come get us, I guess."

Mrs. Entwhistle was unenthusiastic, knowing the price of rescue would be the lecture her son would deliver. She could imagine all too well a long diatribe about how elderly ladies shouldn't go roaming around; look what happened when they did; what a worry and burden she was to her children; her stubborn independence was going to get her killed one day, and yadda, yadda, yadda.

Maxine understood without her friend having to spell it out. She'd known Tommy since he was a baby. "How about Dex?" she asked.

"What would he drive to come get us?" Mrs. Entwhistle said. "All he's got is the scooter. My car isn't even running."

"Why don't we call him anyway and let him know what's happened. He's a very resourceful young man, and he may come up with something we haven't thought of yet."

Dex was properly horrified when he heard Mrs. Entwhistle's story and offered to come get them immediately.

"Driving what? We won't all fit on your scooter," Mrs. Entwhistle reminded him.

"No worries, Mrs. E. Just leave everything to me."

"I will, and I'm very grateful, but don't come today. Maxine is supposed to keep her ankle elevated. We're staying with our friends, the Patels, who are taking wonderful care of us. Tomorrow will be soon enough. Now remember it's an eight-hour drive from home. What are you going to do for wheels?"

"I'll take care of that. You just rest, and I'll see you tomorrow. I'll call from the road and let you know what time I'll be there."

The night was a restless one for Maxine, who couldn't get comfortable. Mrs. Entwhistle didn't sleep well, either, knowing her friend was in pain. If they did manage to doze, they'd be awakened by Dr. Patel. He insisted on checking on his patient every few hours, rattling into the room to shine a flashlight in Maxine's face and take her pulse and blood pressure.

"Please don't disturb yourself," she begged, "it's only a sprain, and I hate for you to lose sleep."

"I will be the judge of what is best for my patient," Dr. Patel said, reigniting Mrs. Entwhistle's simultaneous urges to laugh and smack him a good one.

They woke at sunrise, as was their habit. When Maxine saw Mrs. Entwhistle she popped her hand over her mouth, but she couldn't hold back her laughter. The airbag punch in the face had resulted in two spectacular black eyes.

"I'm sorry; I'm sorry," she gasped, wiping away tears

of mirth. “You look like a raccoon. Oh, I shouldn’t laugh; it’s all my fault.”

Mrs. Entwhistle went to look in the mirror and had to laugh herself. “We’re a fine pair, aren’t we? We’ll make quite an entrance back home, but we’ll mend.”

The ladies managed to get themselves up and dressed before Dr. Patel made his morning visit. He seemed disappointed to find them in good spirits and preparing to leave.

“Ah,” he said when he saw Mrs. Entwhistle’s black eyes. “It’s too late for ice. I would suggest an anti-inflammatory to reduce the swelling.”

He examined Maxine’s ankle, tsk-tsking and shaking his head. “Another day of elevation and rest would be best, but patients are often too quick to get up and around with a sprain,” he said. “I hope you will not do yourself an injury. How is the pain, on a scale of one to ten?”

“My goodness, I don’t know. Four? Five? It hurts a little bit, but it’s no big deal.” Maxine was getting impatient to see about her car and go home.

Dr. Patel reinstated the walking boot and produced a cane, which he insisted Maxine use for balance. It actually wasn’t such a bad idea; she did feel a bit teetery. She thanked him sincerely for his care, and he bowed slightly, nodded his head, turned on his heel and disappeared.

"Great bedside manner, right?" Mrs. Entwhistle said. "Too warm and fuzzy, do you think? Patients will fall in love him."

They were both laughing when the phone rang. It was Dex.

"I'm about an hour out," he said.

"Goodness, what time did you start?" Mrs. Entwhistle asked.

"O-dark-thirty," Dex said cheerfully. "Find out where your car was taken, because we'll have to get your stuff out of it."

Maxine got on the phone and learned that her Lincoln now resided in Fred's Auto Graveyard, which she thought appropriate since her car probably was dead. In any case, she didn't think she ever wanted to drive it again. It had always been too big for her, and she'd only kept it because it was paid for. Now, after experiencing such a frightening accident, she was done with that car.

"I think I'll get me a small model," she said to Mrs. Entwhistle. "Maybe a hybrid. What do you think?"

"Just get one you can see out of without so much

trouble," Mrs. Entwhistle advised. "And one where the seat belts don't choke you."

They made their way to the office to settle their bill, but the Patels wouldn't hear of it.

"No, no, no!" they chorused. "You are our friends and our guests for as long as you wish to stay."

"You're being too kind!" Maxine protested. "You came and got us at the hospital, then your son took such fine care of me, and Anjali made that delicious dinner last night, and ...how can I ever thank you enough?"

"No thanks are necessary, my dear lady," Mr. Patel said.

"You are more than welcome," Mrs. Patel added.

"Well, I hope you'll come and see us someday. I'd love to return the hospitality."

A horn sounded outside and through the window they saw a panel truck with "*The Pantograph*" painted on the side. Dex swung down from the driver's seat and met them at the door with bear hugs and concerned questions. After he'd met the Patels and heard the story of the car wreck again, he explained the truck.

"I made a deal with Mr. McNamara," he said. "I

delivered the morning papers to all the stores in exchange for using the truck. He said to tell you he'll be glad when you're home safe and sound. He would have come himself, but deadlines, you know."

Mrs. Entwhistle nodded, thinking of her editor's naturally indolent nature. No doubt he was having a leisurely plate of pancakes at the Busy Bee Diner at this very moment. Oh, well, it was good to have the truck to haul all their stuff home.

The big Lincoln looked forlorn, setting at an odd angle in the junkyard lot. Maxine could hardly bear to look at the scraped side and door that wouldn't close. Thoughts of what might have been upset her.

"Let's just get our stuff and get out of here," she said.

In a very short time, Dex had transferred the luggage and collected the random items that had spilled out of various bags, and boxes. As he worked, he wore the old straw hat that Mrs. Entwhistle had packed because it made her laugh every time she remembered when Dex wore it to impersonate her. It made her laugh now. Dex could always make her laugh. He stowed everything in the back of the truck, including the hat.

Maxine accepted the price she was offered for her wreck of a car without a murmur. She had insurance, she said, and it would all work out in the end. She began to look forward to purchasing a new car, one that better fit her stature and lifestyle.

Then it was time to think about Marty. "Poor little kitten," Maxine said, dialing Smithers' number and making arrangements to retrieve the cat.

"No, we'll come get him," she said into the phone. "You've done enough. I don't want to put you to any more trouble. We have our dear Dex to drive us now. Just let me know where you live."

Dex got on the phone to listen to the directions, which was a good thing since Smithers lived in a mobile home in the woods. There were no GPS coordinates, only oral directions consisting of "Turn left at the white barn, take a right at the cornfield--no, wait, the farmer's harvested that corn, it's just a stubble field now." When they arrived, Smithers was sitting on the steps waiting for them with Marty in her lap.

Maxine dug in her purse and pulled out some bills. "No way," Smithers said. "I've enjoyed having him. In fact, if you don't want him now that you're injured and all, if you'd find it hard to take care of him... Well, I'd love to take him off your hands."

Maxine smiled and shook her head. "Thank you,

dear, but no. He's just a baby, but we've been through a lot together already. He's my cat, for sure."

"I'll send her a gift certificate to a nice restaurant," she said to Mrs. Entwhistle after they were back in the truck. "Oh, I know! I'll call Randy and pre-pay for two meals at Chez Randy. She can take a friend; maybe Randy'll serve Sex in a Pan. She can't turn that down. Aren't people nice! Think how different our experience would have been without Smithers and the Patels, and now our dear Dex."

"Aw, I bet you talk sweet to all the truck drivers," Dex said.

They rode along in a companionable silence for a few miles, each busy with his or her own thoughts. Then Dex spoke.

"It's going to be an eight-hour ride," he said, "and that should get us home by seven or eight tonight. We'll keep our stops to a minimum, but if you need to get out, and stretch, just say so."

The ladies nodded. They were anxious to get home. Marty purred in his now-clean carrier, his tummy full and the fur on his back shining from all the stroking he'd received under Smithers' hand. Dex maintained a steady speed, and Mrs. Entwhistle felt her eyelids grow heavy. Her head jerked up when

Dex spoke.

"So, Mrs. E., there's something I need to tell you," Dex kept his eyes straight ahead on the highway. He sounded nervous.

"Sure, Dex, what is it?" Mrs. Entwhistle was suddenly wide-awake.

"Well, the thing is, I was pretty cut up when Lara and I split. That's why I wanted to get away from school for a while, you know."

"Yes, and did it help?"

"It did, in a way I never expected. After a while Lara and I started texting a bit, and then we talked, and then we got together and really straightened things out."

"Yes? And?"

"And we're back together. We're going to get married just as soon as we graduate. We can take extra classes and meet all our degree requirements by the end of fall semester. We'll have a Christmas wedding."

"Wow! Dex, I'm so happy for you! Maxine, did you hear that?"

"I sure did. Congratulations, Dex. Lara is a lucky girl.

She couldn't do better if she had her pick of every man on the planet."

"Thanks, but I think I'm the lucky one. Um, there's one more thing." The tips of Dex's ears turned bright pink. "Lara has been staying. With me. At your house. I'm sorry, I know it was presumptuous of me."

There was a pause. Mrs. Entwhistle said, "Is Lara keeping up with her school work?"

"Of course. We're almost finished with our degrees, and we won't let graduation slip away now. She's taking online classes like I am."

"Does Roger like her?"

"Roger loves her."

"Then I don't see a problem," Mrs. Entwhistle said.

"We'll move out now that you're home, of course. I'll try to find a little apartment somewhere."

"Nonsense, you'll do no such thing. I want to get to know Lara, and it'll be a treat for me to have you both around. I get lonely sometimes."

Maxine was surprised at the admission. Mrs. Entwhistle never mentioned being lonely, but Max knew she missed her late husband, Floyd.

Mrs. Entwhistle was fishing around in her big purse. She found what she was looking for and said, "I need you to pull over for a minute."

Dex immediately signaled a turn and parked beside the road. "What's wrong? Do you not feel well?"

"I feel fine. I just want your full attention for this."

She held out a little black velvet box. Maxine caught her breath. It was the ring box from the Cherokee Art Market. Dex opened it, saw the beautiful ring inside and looked at Mrs. Entwhistle questioningly.

"It's for Lara, if you think she'd like it," she said.

"I think she'd love it, but I don't have the money for an engagement ring right now. I couldn't pay you back for a long time."

"Who said anything about paying?" Mrs. Entwhistle asked. "I got it just in case you might need it. I had a feeling you would. Consider it my engagement gift."

Maxine shook her head in wonder. "How did you know to buy it?" she asked Mrs. Entwhistle. "You had no idea Dex and Lara would ever get back together when we were at the Art Market."

"I just... intuited it. You remember when we were at the sweat ceremony, and I said I had a special intention? It was for Dex to be happy again, and I figured that meant with Lara."

"*That* was your special intention? You trusted your intuition enough to buy a ring? What happened to your dislike of 'woo-woo' stuff?"

Mrs. Entwhistle smiled. "Maybe I'm 'woo-woo-ier' than I thought."

What's Happened to You, Jacinta?

The way Maxine drove her new car made Mrs. Entwhistle's right foot hit an imaginary brake from time to time, but she didn't say a word. Let Max have her fun. She'd bought a brand-new car, bright red and sporty, even though the insurance money hadn't come yet.

"It will come in due time," she said airily. "Meanwhile, I need wheels and not a pink scooter, either."

Their homecoming had been joyous, although Roger needed some pampering, including boiled chicken livers for his supper, to recover from the rude shock he'd received. He'd been sniffing the strange new carrier set down on the driveway when a paw reached out and swiped his nose. With a yelp, he turned an indignant face to Mrs. Entwhistle.

"Never mind, Rog, it's just Marty's way. He'll get used to you."

But Roger knew better, due to many bad experiences with the big tomcat next door. He walked away with as much dignity as he could muster and had a long, meditative pee in the backyard. It was a complicated situation for a small dog. He'd have to think it over.

Life gradually returned to normal. They'd done their laundry and picked up their mail at the post office. Groceries were bought and bills were paid. Mrs. Entwhistle cut back her perennials and pulled out her annuals; Dex raked the lawn and burned a huge pile of leaves. The furnace man gave the heating system a going-over and pronounced it ready for another winter. Mrs. Entwhistle felt herself settling cozily back into her routine.

Dex and Lara were proving to be excellent roommates, or boarders, or adopted children – Mrs. Entwhistle wasn't sure just what they were, but she loved them. Lara proudly wore the turquoise ring on the third finger of her left hand, and she and Dex took over most of the household tasks without needing to be asked.

Mrs. Entwhistle resumed her duties at the *Pantograph*, which included editing the weekly column of neighborly gossip and ill-will, the “Palaver.” People sent in their comments under cover of anonymity, making the “Palaver” the newspaper’s most widely-read feature. Human nature being what it was, the submissions were mostly negative and sometimes downright libelous. Speculation about who said what never lost its appeal in the Busy Bee Diner. Fridays, when the “Palaver” ran, meant a full house at breakfast time and a run on the Chef’s Special Biscuits and Gravy.

When Mrs. Entwhistle assembled the e-mails for the column, there was one that made her blood boil. There always seemed to be at least one. This one read, “Some folks have real flexible ideas of right, and wrong. The Bible says, “Be sure your sin will find you out.” She knew it was aimed at her for allowing an unmarried couple to share her home, and she spent a couple of moments in conjecture about who sent it. But then Mrs. Entwhistle decided she didn’t care one whit about other people’s opinions--she was enjoying Lara and Dex too much.

“Judge not, that ye be not judged,” she typed, wishing she could add an emoji face with the tongue sticking out. Technically, she wasn’t supposed to editorialize, but some things couldn't be left unanswered.

Christmas was coming and with it Dex and Lara's wedding. Lara had asked her to be matron of honor, and Mrs. Entwhistle's head buzzed pleasantly with thoughts of what she'd wear, the bridal shower she'd give, and the wedding cake she'd bake. The young couple was having a small, no-frills wedding to fit their budget. Mrs. Entwhistle was determined to add frills any way she could.

These pleasurable pursuits had filled the first days of her homecoming. Now she and Maxine were headed once again to the Shady Rest Assisted Living Center to resume their weekly visits.

"We've got so much to share with them," Maxine said. "I bet they won't even think about their ailments when we start telling them our adventures on Route 66."

The residents sat expectantly in a semi-circle in the day room. Two looked sleepy, but after all, it was early afternoon when many of them were accustomed to napping. Mrs.Entwhistle carried a big batch of Sex in a Pan, and Maxine brought paper plates and plastic forks. They meant to serve it when they got to the part in their travelogue about Chef Randy and the diner in the middle of nowhere. But they had hardly launched into the tale of the Blue Whale when Jacinta interrupted in the loud voice of someone who can't hear well. Mrs. Entwhistle sighed and yielded the floor.

"You know those red pills, the ones I thought were betty blockers? Well, guess what: they aren't betty blockers, they're booty blockers! I asked the doctor to repeat it twice--he mumbles, like all young people do these days--but I'm pretty sure that's what he said. Well, I told him that explains a lot. Sometimes I look in the mirror, and I'm just horrified. I think, what's happened to you, Jacinta? I was Miss Corn Tassel 1958 and now look at me. I blame those booty blockers, and I'll tell you what: I'm going to change doctors!"

ABOUT THE AUTHOR

Doris Reidy believes in second acts. Originally a non-fiction writer, she published articles in *Redbook, Writer's Digest* and *Atlanta Magazine,* among others, along with a monthly book review column for the *Atlanta Journal & Constitution.* After a long literary silence during which life intervened, she reinvented herself as a fiction writer at age seventy. *Mrs. Entwhistle Takes a Road Trip* is the third novel featuring formidable senior citizen, Cora Entwhistle.

Bonus Chapter from
Mrs. Entwhistle

Mrs. Entwhistle Enters the Witness Protection Program

Hanging out her sheets on a sweet, breezy May morning, Mrs. Entwhistle thought with satisfaction that when she climbed into her bed that night, it would smell of springtime. Why would anyone use a dryer on such a day, she wondered, as the crisp cotton pillow cases snapped in the breeze.

Turning to retrieve her cane from where it hung on the clothesline's crossbar, she saw a strange car turn into her driveway. It stopped and disgorged two extremely official-looking personages. They wore matching navy blue windbreakers with such large letters printed on the back that she could read them from across the yard: USMS.

"Swanee," Mrs. Entwhistle said aloud, "What now?"

The strangers' appearance telegraphed law enforcement. She immediately felt guilty, although she couldn't think of anything she'd done wrong. Lately.

"Good morning," she called, wielding her cane carefully as she approached them over the rough spring grass. "Can I help you?"

"Cora Entwhistle?" the male member of the team said, looking down at the papers in his hand.

"Yes, I'm Cora Entwhistle," she replied. "And you are?"

"Deputy Marshall McClellen and Deputy Marshall Seeger of the United States Marshal Service, ma'am," he said, flipping open a leather case to reveal a large gold shield. "We're here to take you to your safe house."

"Take me to what?"

"We've got orders to take you into protective custody. You're in danger, ma'am. Marshall Seeger will help you get your things together, and then we've got to get you out of here. Right now."

"But why? What danger? What about Roger? I can't go anywhere without Roger."

"Roger? We weren't informed of any Roger."

On cue, Roger waddled around the corner of house, gave a desultory bark or two and then sneezed so violently that he had to lie down. Roger didn't get excited about much of anything anymore. He trusted Mrs. Entwhistle to handle whatever needed handling.

"That's Roger, right there," Mrs. Entwhistle said, "and he goes where I go. But why do I have to go anywhere?"

"Ma'am, I can't stress strongly enough the danger of your position. Our orders are to see to it that you stay safe," Marshall McClellen said, fixing her with a steely eye that brooked no nonsense.

Despite her innate contrariness, Mrs. Entwhistle felt a shiver of fear, a ground-fog of confusion and a strong feeling that she'd better obey. She didn't know what they were talking about, but these poker-faced strangers oozed authority and if there was one thing she'd been taught in her youth, it was to respect authority.

"I better call Maxine and ask her to water my plants," she said, looking doubtfully at the newly-planted window boxes.

"You will call no one," Marshall McClellen said. "We'll see to your plants."

Trying for moral outrage, Mrs. Entwhistle thumped her cane on the ground. "Well, for goodness sake," she said, but her voice sounded weak and uncertain to her own ears.

Marshall Seeger, the female half of the team, took Mrs. Entwhistle's arm and steered her firmly toward the house. "Let's get you packed, ma'am. The sooner we can get going, the better," she said.

~*~

Later, Mrs. Entwhistle wondered why she'd submitted so meekly to those bossy strangers. Yes, their badges looked official, but you could probably buy them on the Ultranet, or whatever it was. After a long car ride in which Mrs. Entwhistle had to sit in the back seat behind darkly-tinted windows and all her conversational gambits were met with stony silence, they stopped at a nondescript white frame house on an ordinary suburban street.

"This looks a lot like my street, actually," Mrs. Entwhistle said. The agents did not respond. "Roger probably needs to go out. He's old, he can't wait forever."

"Stay in the car," Deputy Marshall Seeger said. And again, Mrs. Entwhistle did as she was told. She watched the two marshals walk up the path, unlock the door and disappear inside. In five minutes, they were back, opening the car door, motioning for her to get out.

Roger, clipped to his leash, tugged Mrs. Entwhistle to a patch of dusty grass, lifted his leg, lost his balance and settled for a squat. It took him a long time to empty his bladder, and when this was accomplished, he stood blinking up at her, waiting for whatever happened next. She knew how he felt.

Marshalls Seeger and McClellan escorted her into the house. The front door opened directly into a living room furnished with a cheap, imitation leather sectional and a wood-veneer coffee table set against a wall, holding a television set. That was all. The kitchen was equally bare. Mrs. Entwhistle looked around curiously, wondering what all this had to do with her.

"Your bedroom is back here, ma'am," Marshall Seeger said, pointing down a narrow hallway.

"*My* bedroom?" Mrs. Entwhistle said. "No, you are mistaken. I've never been in this house before. I'm ready to go home now."

"This is home for a while, ma'am. You'll be staying here until the trial. There will be a guard posted twenty-four hours a day until then. You'll be perfectly safe as long as no one knows you're here. We strongly caution you to stay inside. You have a phone, but it only takes incoming calls."

"But what about my children? They'll be worried if they can't get me on the phone."

"We've arranged for your calls to be forwarded from your home line. Just don't say where you are when you talk to them. Are they apt to visit?"

"Well…no, not really. We just got together for Diane's birthday last week, so it will be awhile before they come by again. They're so busy, you see, and I don't need their help." She lifted her chin slightly and stared Marshall Seeger in the eye. Nobody was going to get away with the slightest hint of finding fault with Diane and Tommy.

"But what I'd like to know is why I'm here," Mrs. Entwhistle continued. "I don't know anything about a trial. I just want to go home."

"Very convincing," Marshall McClellan said. "You've been well-prepped. You keep that up. There's food in the pantry and an agent in a car at the curb if you need anything."

"I *need* to go *home*," she said, but the agents were already out the door.

~*~

Mrs. Entwhistle was flummoxed. "Roger, what the heck just happened?" she asked. Roger, as was his custom, did not reply. She walked through the house, which consisted of living room, kitchen, bathroom, and two small bedrooms, one of which was unfurnished. It took about two minutes. She stepped out onto the miniscule front porch. At the curb, in a nondescript sedan, sat a young man.

"Yoo-hoo!" Mrs. Entwhistle called. "You out there in the car. Could you come here for a minute?"

The young man hastily exited the car, looking over both shoulders. "Shhhh, ma'am, we don't want to call attention to ourselves," he whispered as he approached.

Mrs. Entwhistle heard only isolated words of this communication. "What?" she asked in her normal tone of voice, which was loud. "I'm sorry, honey, I didn't catch all that."

By now they were at the door and the young man bundled her inside with a firm hand between her shoulder blades. Mrs. Entwhistle mustered her dignity.

"Young man – what is your name, anyway?"

"Deputy Marshall Peters, ma'am."

"Do you have a first name?"

"Yes, ma'am, it's Pete."

"Pete Peters? Peter Peters?"

"Yes, ma'am."

"Well, you poor child. Anyway – Pete. I wanted to ask you and I hope you'll be more informative than your colleagues - what am I doing here? Have I been kidnapped?"

"You're in protective custody until you testify at the trial, ma'am, you know that."

"I *don't* know that. What trial? I don't know anything about a trial or testimony or anything. Those two just came and got me – oh, dear, I left my sheets right on the clothesline, they didn't give me time to think. Now here I am, and I don't know why."

Pete frowned. "I'm really not at liberty to discuss this with you, ma'am. I'm just supposed to make sure you're safe. I'd better get back out to the car now." And he was gone.

Marshalls sure come and go quickly, Mrs. Entwhistle

thought. Roger was looking uneasy, and she thought he probably needed to go out again. The little dog had an old man's bladder and needed frequent forays to the yard. She opened the back door, and they stepped into a tidy but totally uninspired space enclosed by a chain link fence. Roger walked straight to the fence, tail wagging, and greeted a very small human clinging to the other side. *Arf,* he said, meaning, "Here's something interesting. Look, Mom."

Mrs. Entwhistle looked. The child seemed to be no more than two. He or she wore only a diaper, and it was hanging low. Huge brown eyes surrounded by thick lashes peered at her over a thoroughly sucked thumb. She walked over and knelt down, ignoring the protests of her knees.

"Hello, there," she said.

No response. Roger licked the little hands and elicited a squeal. "Doggie, doggie!" the child said.

"His name is Roger. Do you want to pet him?"

A tiny hand reached through the chain link and batted at Roger's nose. He looked delighted at this turn of events, even though he didn't like to have his face touched. Apparently Roger was a pushover for babies. Who knew? There hadn't been any babies in

Mrs. Entwhistle's life since her grandchildren outgrew that stage when Roger was just a pup.

Mrs. Entwhistle looked toward the house next door, hoping to spot the child's mother. That diaper really did need attention. But the house was quiet and shuttered, with no sign of life stirring within or without.

"Where's your mama?" she asked, but the toddler was engrossed with Roger and didn't even glance her way.

"Pete!" she called. Mrs. Entwhistle had a naturally carrying voice. She didn't mean to roar, but often she did without realizing it. "Pete!"

Marshall Peters scurried around the house. "Please, ma'am, keep your voice down."

"Pete, lookey here at this baby out in the yard all alone. What do you make of that? I'm going next door to get its mama. You watch Roger and the baby."

"No, I can't— You can't—"

But Mrs. Entwhistle was gone, plying her cane rapidly over the ground, then using it as a knocker. Repeated thumps brought no response. Meanwhile, the baby's diaper had given up its fight with gravity and was now adorning the grass.

"Well, at least we know it's a boy," Mrs. Entwhistle said. "We can't let him run around naked." She pronounced it *nekkid*. "Pete, you'll have to go to the store for diapers."

Pete began to protest when the little figure at their feet suddenly turned into a fountain.

"Just go on, now," Mrs. Entwhistle said. "You could get in trouble for child neglect."

Although this was clearly illogical, Pete retreated rapidly to his car with hurried instructions that she stay in the backyard, talk to no one, and he'd be right back.

Mrs. Entwhistle and Roger regarded the small figure on the other side of the fence. He was a stocky little boy, and Mrs. Entwhistle didn't think she could lift him up and over the fence. While she wondered what to do, the child toddled to a wide spot in the corner where the two fences met and squeezed through the gap with the nonchalance of repeated practice.

"Well, what about that," Mrs. Entwhistle said. "You little booger, I bet you've done that before. Where in the world is that mama of yours? What's your name?"

But the child was unable or unwilling to reply.

"I'll call you Rocky," Mrs. Entwhistle said, "because it looks like you're between a rock and a hard place, wandering around alone at your age."

Mrs. Entwhistle devised a plan then and there. She'd take advantage of Pete's absence to use a neighbor's phone, notify the police to come and get the baby, call a cab and go home. Simple as that. These marshall people had obviously mistaken her for someone else, but she didn't seem to be having any luck convincing them of that, and she was tired of trying.

"I let myself be intimidated," she said. Talking aloud to herself had become a habit since her husband died. "Shame on me. But I won't continue to be such a spineless sap. I'm going home where I belong."

Pete would be back any minute. She had to hurry. Reaching down, she set the little fellow on his feet, took his hand and set out at his toddling pace to the neighbor's. But they hadn't gotten far when the slam of a car door announced Pete's return. She scurried back into the yard, Rocky and Roger in tow. She barely beat Pete, who arrived peering around the most enormous box of diapers Mrs. Entwhistle had ever seen.

"I went to Costco," Pete explained, reddening under her incredulous gaze. "It was the closest store, and I'm a member."

"Fine, Pete, fine. That ought to take care of Rocky for awhile."

Freshly diapered, the baby began rubbing his eyes and yawning. "He needs a nap. I'm going to make him a pallet on the floor. It's better than nothing," Mrs. Entwhistle said.

Pete scooped up the baby, and they walked toward the house but he stopped so suddenly that Mrs. Entwhistle ran right into the back of him.

"For goodness sake, Pete, watch where—"

Something about the rigid set of Pete's neck made her stop talking. She followed his gaze to a black car with dark windows rolling slowly down the street. The deliberate pace and not being able to see who was inside spoke menace. Pete thrust Rocky at her and said, "Get inside and lock the door behind you. Don't open up for anyone but me."

Gone was the hesitant young man who'd meekly shopped for diapers and in his place stood a steely-eyed lawman. She obeyed. This obedience thing is getting to be a habit, she thought, and look where it's gotten me. She waited meekly, not even daring to peek out of the window, until Pete knocked on the back door.

"It's Deputy Marshall Pete Peters," he said formally. "You can open the door."

"How do I know it's you?" Mrs. Entwhistle asked, not above toying with pompous young people. "Slide your I.D. under the door."

There was a pause, during which she heard Pete muttering. A laminated card slid under the door.

"Okay, then," she said, sliding the dead bolt and turning the knob. "What the heck was all that about?"

"I have orders to move you, ma'am," said Pete, all business.

"Move me where? Why don't you just take me home? And what are you going to do about this baby?"

They both looked down at Rocky, who had fallen asleep on the floor and was drooling into the threadbare carpet. Roger stretched out, exhausted, beside him. Both were snoring lightly. Pete shook his head.

"I don't know," he said.

~*~

In the end, they took Rocky along. Pete said he'd call Child Protective Services as soon as they got to their destination. The baby didn't even wake when he was carried to the car and placed carefully on the back seat.

"You'll get arrested yourself if you get caught with a baby not strapped into a car seat," Mrs. Entwhistle said. She remembered the wild old days when her own children rode rampant, climbing over the seats and sticking their heads out of the windows. Sometimes she'd have to stop the car to spank them when they got too unruly. Car seats were a definite improvement as far as she was concerned.

"It can't be helped. We don't have time for that now. Get in, please."

"Wait. Roger has to go."

"We *are* going."

"No, I mean he has to *go*!"

This took a while, causing Pete to pace and look at his watch, but finally they were underway. Pete's eyes darted between the road ahead and the rearview mirror. Clearly nervous, he made Mrs. Entwhistle nervous. She tried again.

"Look, Pete, just drop me off at my house. I'm not

your witness. There's been a mistake somewhere along the line and you've picked up the wrong person."

But Pete wasn't listening. He'd spotted the black car again, coming up fast behind them. "Hang on!" he said, putting his foot down hard. Rocky slid off the back seat onto the floor and started crying. Roger barked in sympathy. Mrs. Entwhistle turned and tried to reach over the seat to comfort the baby, but the car was rocking and rolling at such speed she couldn't keep her balance.

"Slow down, Pete, you're going to get us all killed," she screamed.

"That's exactly what I'm trying to avoid!"

Pete executed a series of hairpin turns, darted through a red light and zipped through an alley so narrow that he left the passenger mirror behind. Spotting an open garage, he drove in, jumped out and punched the button that closed the door. They all blinked in the sudden gloom, and even Rocky stopped crying and stuck his thumb in his mouth.

Mrs. Entwhistle broke the silence. "Do you know these people?" she asked.

"You mean the people whose garage this is? Whose house we're sort of breaking into and entering?

Why, no, I do not."

Pete had a wild look in his eyes and seemed on the verge of hysterics. Mrs. Entwhistle recognized that look as the same one Tommy used to get when he became overwrought. No good ever came of giving in to that, she knew, so she spoke firmly.

"Well, all right, then. I'm sure they'll understand that it was an emergency. They're probably all at work anyway--"

She broke off in mid-sentence as the door connected to the house flew open, revealing a very young boy holding a very big gun. It was pointed directly at Mrs. Entwhistle.

"Stop, or I'll shoot!" the boy said. "I called 911, and the cops will be here any minute, so don't you try nothin'."

Mrs. Entwhistle was annoyed. She'd had about all the aggravation she could handle in one twenty-four hour period, and the day was far from over.

"You put that gun down this minute, young man," she said. "You might hurt yourself, and you know very well you are not allowed to touch any of your father's guns when he's not home." She didn't realize she was roaring.

"It's not real," the boy said. "It's just a rep-repi-ca, my Dad said. But it looks real, don't it?" He dropped the gun with a plasticky clatter.

"That's better. Now we'd like to come in before the police get here, if you don't mind. We've got this baby, you see."

She looked around for Rocky, but he was heading into the house with the assurance of one who'd been there before. The resident boy looked at the toddling boy with astonishment.

"Joey? What are you doing here?" he said.

"Do you know this baby?" Mrs. Entwhistle said.

"Sure, that's Joey. He's my sister's baby. Why do you have him?"

"Pete, where are we? Surely, we're far from where this baby belongs," Mrs. Entwhistle said.

"Actually, we made a big circle getting away from the car that was following us. We're on the back side of the block where the safe house is," Pete said.

"And you know this baby?" Mrs. Entwhistle said again.

"Like I said, that's my nephew, Joey. Where's my sister? She works nights, but her boyfriend watches

Joey while she sleeps."

"Nobody was watching him when I found him," Mrs. Entwhistle said grimly. "Anybody could have taken him. Lucky for him it was me."

"I'd better call my sister. She'll go nuts if Joey's not there when she wakes up."

"You can't call anyone, son," Pete said, clearing his throat and squaring his shoulders. "You're officially under the protection of the U.S. Marshall Service now, and I can't allow communication on any device."

"She probably wouldn't hear the phone anyway. She sleeps like she's dead," the boy said. "But you better get Joey back to her before she misses him, or I'm not kidding, she'll go nuts."

"What's your name, young man?" Mrs. Entwhistle inquired.

"Jack."

"Pleased to meet you, Jack. I'm Mrs. Entwhistle, and this is Marshall Peters. He's a good guy, so don't be scared."

Pete looked like he was scared, himself. In fact, he looked like he was about to cry. Mrs. Entwhistle gave him a reassuring thump on the back. Pete jumped a foot at the unexpected touch and whirled around to see who was attacking him. Mrs. Entwhistle ignored this display of nerves. He was a grown man and a government agent, after all. In her opinion, he was responsible for this whole mess, and he could just darn well buck up. However, since he was clearly in a vulnerable state, it might not hurt to try to influence him again.

"It's time for you to take me home now, Pete," she said with all the authority of her seventy-eight years. She looked him straight in the eye, a double death-ray Mom Glare. Predictably, he quailed before it.

"Ma'am, I really can't do that," he said miserably.

"Pete, there's been a bad mistake made somewhere up the line. Not you, you're just following orders. But somebody has got me mixed up with the real witness in this trial you keep talking about. That person might be in danger right now, but you're protecting *me*. What if, while you're protecting the wrong person, the right person gets hurt? Whose record would that go on? I'm betting yours, not the big bosses. Am I right?"

"You're right about that part, anyway," Pete said. "But I can't just countermand an order when I'm out in the field."

"This is your chance to show you have initiative – leadership. I bet you'll be a hero. After all, I'm being held against my will. I believe that's called kidnapping. Again, who do you think will take the blame for that? You need to drop me off at home, and then go and get this whole thing straightened out."

"But what about the baby? We can't just leave these kids alone."

"Jack, what time will your parents be home?" Mrs. Entwhistle asked.

"Not until five-thirty," Jack said. "But Joey and me could go to my sister's house. She'll wake up if I shake her good. Then when my folks come home, she can bring me home. Oh boy, she's going to be in truuuuuuuble!"

Pete wiped a hand over his tired face as he thought over his options. He suddenly looked very young. Mrs. Entwhistle waited in silence. She knew enough about men to know you can only push so far.

"Look, I have to check in with headquarters," he finally said.

"You already know what they'll say," Mrs. Entwhistle said. "You're in this mess because you're following orders from people that have got it wrong."

Pete looked pained. He paced. He gazed out the window. Finally, he turned to Mrs. Entwhistle with a look of resolve.

"You're right," he said. "Let's get you home. I'll deal with the consequences."

~*~

Mrs. Entwhistle's house looked different, somehow. She felt as though she'd been gone for days instead of a few hours. Not a soul stirred on her street. Doors and windows wore a shuttered, unfriendly look. Pete helped her out of the car, holding Roger's leash while she paused for a moment to give her knees time to decide to move. Later she thought if she'd had younger knees, Pete wouldn't have gotten shot.

The same car with the ominously-tinted windows came screeching around the corner and then everything happened at once. Pete shoved her back into the car so hard that she fell full length across the front seat, whacking her head hard on the steering wheel. Roger let out an indignant yelp as Pete stepped on his tail. There was a sound like a car back-firing, and Mrs. Entwhistle felt little glass pellets rain down upon her. Then the car was gone.

With difficulty, she pulled herself up, head spinning,

and brushed the glass out of her hair. But where was Pete? Roger's rusty bark directed her gaze downward, and she saw him, lying half under the car on his back in a horrifying pool of dark red blood. Mrs. Entwhistle pressed her hands to her spinning head and willed the world to hold still. She knelt beside Pete.

"Pete! Peter Peters," she said, her voice even louder than usual because she was scared.

Pete's eyes opened, but they looked glassy and uncomprehending. "Don't you die, now, you hear me? Don't be ridiculous. You're going to be all right."

Neighbors were coming out of their houses, gathering around the car. Several people were on their cell phones calling 911. Pete gave a long sigh and then – nothing. Without pausing to think, Mrs. Entwhistle tipped his head back, opened his mouth, bent over and blew a long steady breath into his mouth. She waited a few seconds and did it again, rewarded this time by the sight of Pete's chest rising. Pressing the heels of her hands into his sternum, she began rapid compressions.

Through the adrenalin rush that possessed her senses, she heard the sirens coming closer. Time stopped as she concentrated on counting rapidly to one hundred, her hands keeping time. In a few seconds or a few days, strong hands lifted her out of the way, and blue-uniformed paramedics took over. One continued compressions while two more lifted Pete onto a stretcher and into the back of the ambulance. Mrs. Entwhistle sat on the grass beside Roger, suddenly feeling that her legs wouldn't hold her. Ronnie Sue from next door helped her to her feet and retrieved her cane from where it fallen in the street. She walked slowly to her door.

"Come on, Roger," she said. "We're home."

~*~

"So then what happened?" Maxine asked, breathless with second-hand excitement. She'd rushed right over with homemade vegetable soup when Mrs. Entwhistle called. Maxine believed in the restorative powers of soup and always had a pot simmering. "And how did you know how to do CPR, anyway? Did you take a course?"

Mrs. Entwhistle shook her head. "But I watch a lot of television – cop shows, you know. Saw it done a hundred times. Nothing to it, really," she said modestly.

"And will Pete be okay?"

"So they tell me. He's getting some kind of a medal for saving my life, and I'm invited to the ceremony as soon as he gets up and around. Just between us, Maxine, I think I saved his life just as much as he did mine. It seems to me I should get a medal, too, but those Marshalls are trying to forget I ever existed. They're just hoping I won't sue them for false arrest or something. Which I could, maybe, but I won't. Life's too short for that kind of aggravation."

"What about the real witness?" Maxine asked.

"It's all a big secret until after the trial. When those television guys came around I looked right into the camera and said that Cora Entwhistle is not a material witness to anything. Do you think I'll be on the eleven o'clock news tonight?"

"Probably," Maxine said. "Let's stay up late and watch it together."

"Diane and Tommy will have a hissy fit if they see me on the news before I've told them about it" Mrs. Entwhistle said. "And I know what's coming: lectures about staying home and keeping out of trouble. How was it *my* fault, I'll say to them. I was just hanging out sheets, minding my own business."

"For a change," Maxine said with a wink. "What about those little kids?"

"That naked baby and gun-toting little boy? They're all right, although I bet that baby's mama got a good scolding from her own mama for letting him wander. 'Boyfriend was watching him', indeed," she said with a snort. "Boyfriends typically don't make very good baby-sitters; you'd think women would figure that out."

Maxine nodded with pursed lips. She and Mrs. Entwhistle could go on for hours about the general stupidity and ineptitude of the younger generation.

"I'll tell you one thing, Maxine," Mrs. Entwhistle said, "being in witness protection is a wearisome task. It just flat tuckers a person out. Come on and help me get my sheets in off the line before it gets dark. Aren't they going to smell good, after a whole day in the sunshine!"

Made in the USA
Columbia, SC
30 September 2023

23654641R00157